D0145361

A LAUGHING PLACE

A LAUGHING PLACE

*The Art and Psychology of
Positive Humor
in Love and Adversity*

by

Christian Hageseth III, M.D.

Berwick Publishing Company
Fort Collins, Colorado

Typesetting by Patrick Shuck of Teletech

Printed in the United States of America
        Citizen's Printing Company
        Fort Collins, Colorado

Cover Design by Paul Jensen

Library of Congress Catalog Card Number: 88–71210

ISBN 0-9620639-0-8

First Printing, July 1988
Second Printing, December 1988
Third Printing, November 1989

Berwick Publishing Company
501 Spinnaker Lane
Fort Collins, Colorado 80525

For Carol

CONTENTS

Acknowledgements

Every author knows he is but part of a process that culminates in a book being published. Starting with childhood, the list of acknowledgements could read like an autobiography. Recalling influential persons always carries the risk of leaving some out. I hope to avoid such a pitfall, but apologize in advance if I should fail.

The most significant person in my humor development was my father, Christian J. Hageseth. With only an eighth grade education and The Great Depression to support him, he managed a life of considerable poverty as a travelling salesman, selling automotive parts over the western half of North Dakota. Never did I see him use humor to harm another. All who knew him were moved by his extraordinarily good-natured humor and gentle wit.

My brother and sister were my first companions in humor and adversity. Together we weathered some storms. And together we shared some wonderful laughter. Both have offered me support in this endeavor. I am grateful for their encouragement.

My children have convinced me that humor is essential to the enterprize of being a parent. It may be the single best antidote for parent burn-out. Right now they don't think Dad is too funny, but I hope one day they will. My experience with them

9

has taught me the central role of humor in parent/child bonding. Sharing laughter with them has brought me joy.

In my extended family are the Medalen's of Willow City, North Dakota. Since the forties they have known more adversity than any other ten families I know. Yet, they have maintained dignity, loving attachment, faith, and an indomitable sense of humor. All who know them appreciate their strength of purpose and their good-natured humor.

C. W. Metcalf started this humor business with me and stimulated my creativity. Together we developed much of the material underlying the theory of positive humor. Thanks, C.W.

My writing skills have been refined and nurtured by Carolyn Duff who has painstakingly reviewed my wandering prose and helped it become a bit more disciplined. I would never have succeeded without her help.

My friends at Interface have been like a family to me. Their support and friendship have sustained me for years. If they doubted I would ever complete this project, they never let me know. Thanks to Phyllis Moody, Bev O'Connor, Carl Spina, Lowell Jenkins, Don Fish, Tally Scott, Andrea Anderson, Allen Brandon, and Collyer Ekholm.

A scattering of other wonderful friends supported my work when it lagged and laughed when I played the clown. Ron and Margaret Taunt, Ezra and Evelyn Sheffres, Karen Cushman, Fred and Nancy Brigham, Mark Sloniker, Larry Kennedy (my primary joke supplier) and Jim Disney. Thanks.

My Friends of the Fort Collins Silent Meeting shared the Light with warmth and occasional laughter. With them, my spirit found a safe place to rest.

And finally, one person has opened my being so fully, that my creativity could sing. She proved my search for love was not an adolescent neurosis. She demonstrates that God comes to us within the being of those who love us. She always laughs with me and encourages my often feeble attempts at humor. She has read every revision of every chapter and never once failed to encourage me. Lucky am I that she is spending life with me. I dedicate this book, with grateful thanks to my wife, Carol Joy Nees.

Preface

       This book will teach you how and why to incorporate humor in your life. It has its funny moments, but it is not a book about comedy—rather, it is primarily a book about life, stress, and adversity—*and* a book about humor, love, and spiritual growth. In the contemporary mind, humor is similar to the weather: Everyone wants to change it, but nobody is quite sure how. The central concept of positive humor requires you take yourself lightly while you take your work-in-life seriously. Then you can learn and practice non-verbal humor stimulation, play with forbidden topics, and finally, tell a joke or two. The theory of positive humor provides the basis for improving your own sense of humor and encouraging a similar change for loved ones or co-workers. The techniques and applications which follow the theory chapters may surprise the reader who still holds the mistaken notion that jokes are the primary mechanism for creating humor.

       In its unique approach to the psychology of humor, this book suggests positive humor as a central process to parent/infant bonding. While most humor theorists constantly look for aggression behind all humor attempts, this approach looks for the loving intent behind such efforts. From time immemorial, humor has been used aggressively and has supplied a weapon for psychological warfare in families and in society. At the same time, humor has served as comic relief in the midst of adversity and has provided a loving communication process for all humanity. Hence it is necessary to distinguish positive [loving, healing] humor from negative [aggressive, destructive] humor. Since the world abounds with hostility, *A Laughing Place* emphasizes how to apply humor lovingly.

The techniques and applications of this book present easy-to-follow "how to's" for developing humor in your life. However, if you have not understood the preceding chapters—or, worse yet, skipped over them entirely—the behavioral material will appear elementary or unsophisticated. Hence, the book is best read from start to finish. Thereafter, you can use the applications section as you would a cookbook, modifying the content to meet your specific needs.

The case histories are examples of life, adversity, and humor. They are true, many coming directly from my twenty years of experience as a physician and psychiatrist. In all cases, however, the anonymity of my patients is maintained. I have modified names, places, and situations but the essential underlying features remain true to the lives they represent.

The choice of gender in pronoun usage does not have any rhyme or reason. Whether it is "him" or "her" depended on my whim at the moment. When in doubt, I flipped a coin. In the most gnarly situations, the gender of a given pronoun was referred to a committee made up of Mohammed Ali, Gloria Steinem, and James Watt. If you think some particular pronoun usage is sexist, please forward your criticism to one of the committee members.

This book is intended for a wide general audience. If you have ever been a parent or a child, you qualify. The style is intentionally informal and even conversational, but definitely not frivolous. The content addresses humor in depression, physical illness, grief, and high-level wellness—all appropriate concerns in every person's life. The psychology portion presents how humor is acquired and lost through growth and development from cradle to grave. The ultimate purpose is to help you experience a life with more love, more laughter, and less pain. Best wishes as you enter the world of the zygomaticus major and gelastolalia.

A LAUGHING PLACE

CHAPTER I

The Fly

Allow me to introduce myself

Four minutes to show time. I'm not nervous but at the moment I'm doing what every male public speaker must do before standing in front of an audience. I'm in the men's room. The final primping, the deep breaths. Making sure my thin hair is just so. I thought my evolving baldness would cure my cowlick problem. It didn't.

C.W., my partner, is in the stall meditating his way through a cigarette. It is the only place he can smoke in the medical center that is hosting the workshop. There are no other men in the room, but I respect the silence just in case the feet I see don't belong to who I think they belong to. Terribly embarrassing to start a conversation with the guy in the stall just to find out you don't know him.

Three local TV channels and two newspapers are here. Well, I'm ready. But as I make my final checks I run into a glitch. Just as I lock my zipper into the up and stowed position, the little metal flipper comes off in my hand. I look down and discover my fly is—as we said in the military—FUBAR ("fouled" up beyond all repair). The once interlocking twin sides recoil from each other in snarly contortions. How it happened, I don't know. But who has time to worry about cause now? I have emergency repairs to attend to. Damage control so to speak. It is nine o'clock sharp and I believe in being punctual.

I adjust my tie so the long end is really long. I walk out in the hall stooping forward slightly and catch the nearest nurse. Physicians are used to nurses bailing them out of all sorts of jams. Though, as a psychiatrist, I am not considered a "real doctor" anymore, I still appreciate the help nurses provide in time of need.

"Nurse..."

"Yes?"

"I have a problem." I straighten my posture enough for the end of my tie to ascend to the level of my belt buckle.

"You certainly do."

Nurses can be so business like. Especially when you depend on them. No silly business. No, Ma'am. She returns with a faint smile and half a wink—I think she recognizes me from the brochure—and two safety pins.

"Thank you."

"Don't mention it." Her twinkle belies her hunch that this was just part of the performance.

Three minutes after nine and I have serious work to do. I return to the sanctity of the men's room. It is good there are private places for dealing with private matters.

Now, I don't know how you measure the size of safety pins. But being a doctor, I do know about hypodermic needles. Twenty-eight gauge are tiny ones for allergy shots and the like, mere mosquito bites. Twenty-two gauge needles are for your average hypos. Sixteen gauge needles are those garden hoses they use for drawing off a pint of blood. Well, the nurse had given me two silver safety pins, both sixteen gauge.

As I work on my dilemma, something else becomes clear to me—besides the fact I had gained ten pounds in the last few months—men in our culture have never been taught how to pin anything from the inside so the pin doesn't show. Women learn that skill in their earliest childhood. They start with dolls and regularly use safety pins to snug up necessities well into adult life. I have pinned my share of diapers, but you don't care if the pins show; you just don't want the darn things to fall off.

16

The Fly

Anymore you don't even need pins, it's all adhesive tape.

Feeling like a contortionist, I use body English and facial expressions to help. But to no avail. It is eight minutes after nine, and C.W. is through meditating. He comes out and washes his hands. He smiles. "What's up, Doc? Got a little fly problem?"

"Charlie," (I call him Charlie most of the time), "This is no joke. My fly is history."

First he rolls his eyes but then he realizes I'm not joking. He gets serious. "Here, let me see."

To get a better view of things, he kneels in front of me. He puts on his reading glasses to focus better at close range and tips his head back to see through them. Together, he and I try using our four hands to hold the zipper edges next to each other, and then try to affix the safety pins from the inside.

Three men walk in talking and laughing. I assume they want to use the rest room. But for some reason they don't stay. They get real quiet. They turn and leave the room without a word. I wonder if they were coming to the workshop.

"I can't do it, doc."

"Aw, to hell with it." I fasten the two pins diaper style and just let them hang out. We go on stage ten minutes late.

I start: "If Richard Nixon had just been honest at the beginning of Watergate, he would never have ended up in so much trouble. Here I stand before you to tell you that we are late getting started because my fly just broke."

Charlie helps by directing attention to the silver pins. The audience thinks it's a gag. A portable TV camera sweeps down from the rear of the auditorium and does a close up of my pin job. Laughing, everybody thinks it's part of the show. In fact, my efforts to convince them of my honesty only serve to make them all the more certain.

I never have been a big fan of TV journalism. And that night, my fly was a fleeting feature on the local evening news.

Given: Living will guarantee you adversity. The only question is how to deal with it. When you get embarrassed, you can withdraw, cry, hit, develop ulcers, or even die. Or, on occasion, you can employ humor. That morning I decided to use humor instead of delaying the show, having a migraine, or getting angry with the clothing manufacturer. More often than not, humor will carry you through life's embarrassing moments. It will also help you deal with grief, interpersonal strife, marital conflict, workplace stress, life threatening illness, baldness, excess adipose, and teenage children. It will not help you with end-stage depression, Ralph Nader, or the IRS.

Since 1983 I have been presenting workshops on the use of humor. The participants have included doctors, nurses, teachers, therapists, bankers, farmers, clergy, police, military personnel, businesspersons, and plain old average folks. The response is the same everywhere. Ninety-eight percent believe humor is an essential ingredient of their mental health. Ninety percent believe humor is important to maintaining physical health. Less than two percent remember and tell jokes well, while over ninety percent believe they have a reasonably good sense of humor. Ninety-five percent want an improved sense of humor. And one hundred percent wish their spouses or co-workers would improve their senses of humor.

Despite numerous books on humor, none contains information that tells you how to improve your overall sense of humor. Many will tell you humor is good for you. Others will be funny to read and entertain you in the process. Some will scientifically examine humor, leaving it dead and—like a dissected frog—spread out on the table. None accurately portrays the pain of living and demonstrates why humor exists and how it truly allows you to survive and grow through adversity. I believe it is possible to alter your perspective on life and change your behavior so humor will be more accessible and successful.

You can best understand humor's value in your life if you see humor in relation to adversity. You may want to ignore adversity, but life will not allow you this posture. It is through adversity that we learn the value of humor. Not just a trivial ornament appended to the human psyche, humor is a vehicle that bears us through the pain of life, its disappointments, its losses, and its cruelty.

18

As I participated in the painful lives of the patients in my psychiatric practice, I saw they needed more than relief from psychological pain; they needed to work and to love and to laugh. Psychiatry is tough work. There were times we could accomplish no more than symptom removal and resignation. I began to burn out; my compassion began to wane, and I began to dwell in the darkness of depression in all its varied forms.

Then, not by coincidence, I found myself teaching what I most needed to learn—the art and psychology of positive humor. I didn't just want to treat the aftermath of adversity; I wanted to prevent some of the pain that was poured out in my consulting room. People are frequently very cruel to each other. Perhaps I could teach them how to be more loving and playful instead. An ounce of humor properly applied might prevent a pound of therapy at some later date. Most of my patients succeeded at work, but few achieved love or laughter.

Though love in all its forms—be it romantic, parent-child, friendship, or agape—is the ultimate prevention of psychological ills, the practice of love is difficult to teach. The contemporary mind seriously confuses the meaning of love and often perverts loving behaviors. Humor is equally misunderstood. Just as people see love as merely a feeling to be indulged when it feels good, they understand humor as comedy with little relevance to their intimate relationships or careers. Comedy is rarely constructive. More often it is cynical, rude, and aggressive. Teaching comedy doesn't teach love; on the contrary, comedy's negative humor may destroy love. The solution to the dilemma posed by these overlapping confusions is to blend true humor with healthy love. The result: Positive humor.

Though more art than psychology goes into the blending process, psychology makes the subject more systematic and easier to learn. In our quasi-scientific world, psychology provides credibility. Art allows for creativity and fun. In our repetitive and pre-packaged world, art provides the means for the human spirit to soar and to play.

CHAPTER II

In A Nutshell

What this book is about

Doctor, in thirty seconds tell us about humor. What do you tell people that they don't already know? Aren't there people who never laugh? Can you really learn to have a sense of humor? Isn't humor really just a form of aggression that has been modified? Is it true that by laughing people can cure themselves of cancer? Will an improved sense of humor be reflected in "the bottom line"? Will a corporation that rewards humor really make more money? Do you have any conclusive proof that laughing will make people live longer? Thank you, doctor, and how do you pronounce your last name? What nationality is that?

A poet was once asked to interpret one of his poems. He replied something like, "You ask me to say in other words what I spent two years attempting to say perfectly by the very words in that poem?" But news media demand crisp, to-the-point comments. The thirty-second-spot is a reality we all have to live with. The length of many magazine articles is determined by how long people sit in the rest room. So here is what I have to say about humor, without detail, without examples, without metaphor. Those will come later.

1. Humor is an innate human quality. Its potential is present in all human beings regardless of intelligence, culture, or education. Since it is ubiquitous, it must be very important. Rather than being some superfluous part of the human psyche, it is essential. In fact, psychopathology is often characterized by an absence or perversion of humor.

2. Humor is constantly being modified by life experience. Life's adversity and the Western work ethic generally conspire to minimize the expression of humor. But if you can be persuaded to see humor as an asset, you will experience its benefits in an enhanced quality of life. You can transform humor into a positive and helpful skill. You can improve your sense of humor. You need only be motivated—persuaded that it is in your best interest—and be given reasonable instructions how to go about it.

3. Humor in its original form is loving, not aggressive. Aggression is acquired later than humor, which is first manifested in the smiling response at about eight weeks of age. There is no question that humor can be used aggressively and can be very harmful. But its first function in life is to convey human love. Its ideal use throughout life is to express love, not aggression. Hence, it is possible to distinguish positive from negative humor. You can learn the difference and then accentuate the positive and eliminate the negative. Such a goal is reasonable and achievable by the average person.

4. The use of positive humor favors mental and physical health. Beyond merely protecting you from illness, positive humor enhances wellness. That is not to say that if you laugh all the time you will never have to see another doctor. If you live that idea, you will probably die laughing.

5. Humor and creativity utilize similar brain processes. To foster creativity, humor must be nurtured, not stifled. In the short run, avoiding humor seems to increase productivity, but that is like growing a crop in the same soil without ever adding

fertilizer. The profit in the first few years looks better, but later on the soil is exhausted and will fail to grow even marginal crops. In the long run, a prohibition of humor is a prohibition of creativity.

6. Humor must be balanced. It is possible to get too much of a good thing. There are times and places where humor is not appropriate. Humor used in excess is negative just as its thoughtless use in certain settings can be cruel and harmful.

7. Positive humor reduces stress and enhances communication. Hence it is good for any enterprize that depends on communication. Health, wellness, and productivity are all enhanced by the appropriate and timely use of positive humor. When humor enters the work environment, employee morale and creativity improve; sick time decreases.

8. Humor shared within a family comprises one of the most powerful parenting techniques known. Properly used, it may eliminate the need for tough love at a later time.

9. Humor within a marriage may be more loving, even, than sex. Of course, when the two are experienced concurrently, a whole new dimension of both laughter and sexuality may be discovered. Could we get just a little less serious about sexual aerobics? The couple that laughs together....

10. Humor is a broad concept, including a way of perceiving life and behavior that is congruent with that perception. It is more than jokes; it accompanies every forbidden thought that might creep through your mind and feeds upon every expressive behavior from the faintest smile to all-out, slap-your-sides laughter. Learning positive humor will involve changing both your behavior and your perceptions. Humor requires you to take risks and so you will have to take yourself a good deal more lightly than may be your custom.

A principle in medicine is *primum non nocere*: First of all, do no harm. Medicine must do no harm before it seeks to help the condition it is intended to treat. Some psychological prescriptions in recent years fail to follow this dictum. The cult-like worship of the self often causes others to pay for your supposed psychological growth. Humor applied indiscriminately may cause harm. Negative humor clearly causes harm. Positive humor will not harm. It will promote love, healing, and creativity. It is good medicine. And it is free. Just as your own immune system is your best defense against infections and cancer, so too is humor among your best psychological defenses for life's adversity. Depression impairs your immune system leaving you more vulnerable to disease. Suppression of humor impairs you as well, making you more vulnerable to depression and disease.

Our world suffers from a lack of positive humor on a global scale. I wish the leaders of the world would learn and practice positive humor. But I don't have much influence on world leaders. (Does any of us?). But I do know how to help individuals change: Clear up the garbage that has accumulated in life, let the innate human capacity for growth proceed, then guide and educate the process of growth as it goes along. Perhaps the way to change the world is by teaching one individual at a time.

CHAPTER III

Life Is Difficult

How I Came To Teach Positive Humor

My practice was bulging at the seams with suicidal people, incest victims, and some tormented souls who believed themselves to be possessed. The threat of suicide was my daily companion. Stories of abuse saddened me and gradually twisted my perception till I couldn't see a father and daughter walking together without muttering "incest" under my breath. I looked into the subject of human evil with considerable fear and some foolish abandon. I grudgingly learned that some people consciously sought to please the archetype of Satan as they understood it. At just that moment, the Wisdom behind the universe saw a need for balance in my life and introduced me to mirthful humor—a road too seldom travelled by many who suffer life's misfortunes.

Actually, as I look back, my use of positive humor started long ago. Probably in my early childhood when I survived my mother's disabling mental illness and narcotics addiction. My brother, my sister, and I formed our own humor support group. We joked a lot. We laughed with Jack Benny and Bob Hope on the radio. We played word games while we washed dishes or cleaned house. We developed silent eye contact understandings and word intonations that went over our mother's head and protected us from her frequent abuse. We learned to avoid feeling offended when people discovered she was in the mental hospital. We used our humor to displace our shame. It brought some light into the dark depression that was our home.

During adult life, my humor experience grew almost imperceptibly as I moved through my medical career. Actually, I have tried about five different careers in medicine. After sampling the first four, I became a psychiatrist. I started out planning to be a pediatrician. I completed a year of internship in pediatrics before entering the Navy where I studied aerospace medicine. The draft and my own patriotism dictated I volunteer—after all, there was a war on. It wasn't much of a war, but it was the only one at the time. Studying aerospace medicine prepared me to become a "Flight Surgeon." That title, Flight Surgeon, is a little bit of a joke in itself. We fly some, but are not pilots. And we do no surgery *per se*. We take care of the healthiest specimens on the face of the earth to make sure they are physically and mentally fit for the rigors of flight.

I found myself spending the Viet Nam war on the East Coast at a Marine Corps Air Station. I spent half my time as a flight surgeon and the other half as a pediatrician. Instead of demonstrating against the war, I took care of the men before they went to war. And I cared for the families of those men. Those who went to war and those who didn't come back. I played with the toys of war. I spent some of the most unusual days imaginable. During a morning, I might fly "second seat" in a high performance jet aircraft and drop napalm on wrecked tanks and trucks. Then I would come home for lunch, change my clothes, and return to the pediatric clinic where I would perform well-baby examinations on infants six to eighteen weeks of age. I would spend the morning discussing dive angles, release altitudes, and armament configurations. I would spend the afternoon discussing immunizations, infant formulas, and diaper rash. Remaining good-natured in this life of contrast didn't seem to be merely an option, it seemed essential to my sanity.

The Marines and their families have wonderful senses of humor. Many friendships I made back then continue to the present day, even though I am now a Quaker and disavow war and preparations for war. However, it seems when war is your unspoken companion, you quickly discover that you must balance your mind and protect yourself against the inevitable madness that would come from dwelling on the subject. Anybody who has known military people personally knows that most of them have wonderful senses of humor. They maintain their humor to survive.

After my military years, I was still undecided about a specialty, so I spent some time in general practice and worked in an emergency room in Washington state. I was in a middle sized community on the banks of the Columbia River with a marvelous view of Mount St. Helens. Of course, nobody had heard of it in those days. It was just another pretty, dormant volcano. One night in the emergency room an event occurred that moved me towards psychiatry and ultimately towards humor work. At the time, I didn't exactly see it that way.

Two A.M. monday morning. Usually a quiet time in an ER. A time to snatch a little sleep and hope that maybe it will be a quiet night. Rather than napping that night, I was gossiping with Barb, the night nurse. It was just the two of us. Opal, the night supervisor—a banti hen if ever there was one—would come if we needed an extra nurse, and an orderly would be floated to us if we got too busy. The security guard came around every half hour or so and talked about his varicose veins.

Emergency medicine is a little like flying; hours of boredom punctuated by moments of stark terror. The radio interrupted our talk time. "We got a bad one and we're coming in. Gunshot wound in the face. We are doing CPR. We have a pulse but no BP. We're breathing him with a mask but we don't have much of an airway. We'll be there in seven minutes....or less."

Anticipate, anticipate, anticipate. Plan, set up the room. Call the other staff and calm yourself. Go outside, maybe you can hear the siren. Keep cool. Don't think of too many specifics. Be ready for anything. No TV cameras like Ben Casey. Just real life and real death. They cut the siren a block away (Don't wake up the patients who are asleep). As they come up the driveway, they cut the flashing red lights, too.

I have always believed that the leader of an emergency team does a better job when he speaks quietly and moves deliberately. It keeps everybody efficient and prevents accidents like dropping IV bottles or worse yet, bodies. As I silently greet them, the two attendants fix me with a quick glance while removing the stretcher. Their pursed lips and slight shake of their heads convince me this *is* a bad one. The blood on their hands does too.

A young man is on the cart. He has shoulder length, stringy black hair, thick and matted with blood. His bearded face is distorted and bloody. Keep the CPR going. Airway, airway, airway. Then circulation. Deal with other matters later. I've seen a tracheotomy about five times in my career. You're supposed to anticipate it and let a specialist do it whenever possible. No specialists tonight. Just me. I'm it. Barb knows it too. The pack is open. All the instruments are there. I do it and *voila*, it works. Now we can really breathe for him.

Stop the massage and see what his heart does by itself. Look at the EKG. Yes, it's beating. It's slow, but it is beating. Good deal, we might save him. Now it's time to look elsewhere. Call lab, call X-ray. Assess the rest of the situation. Barb and Opal both pat me on the back, complimenting my surgical skill. I smile and mention it is my first solo tracheotomy.

Blood loss is the concern now. Wound of entry and wound of exit, where are they? I have a moment, and so I ask the policemen about the circumstances—there are three in the room by now. "Not good, Doc. The kid did it to himself. Had an argument with his mother and his girlfriend. He used a 30-06."

Oh, shit! That's a lot of gun. Where is the wound of entrance? There, under the jaw. No wonder the airway was impossible. The tongue and mouth are just like so much hamburger. One eye is slightly extruded. No time for nausea. Just get the work done. Where is the wound of exit? If he did it to himself, he must have pointed the rifle upwards. That means the exit wound is probably on the top of his head. In the long matted hair I feel for the top of the cranial vault. Much of it is missing. It is all squishy. All over. His brain is destroyed, FUBAR.

28

I look up at my friends. In this moment, they aren't just co-workers, they are friends. He's dead. We have an airway and an EKG, but no brain. Stop breathing for him. Disconnect the EKG. I don't want to watch it stop. I motion for Opal to stop squeezing the bag. We stand in silence. We exhale slowly and let our shoulders drop. The X-ray and lab techs arrive just in time to see Barb pull out the IV. They ask if we want them. We say no, but thanks.

As I walk out, the police are in the hall with the mother and the girlfriend. I never soft soap news of death. I never use cliches. I always touch the people I talk to and I always look in their eyes.

"He's dead. The wound was fatal from the moment he pulled the trigger. There is nothing that could save him. Not now." I look at each of them. I wish it wasn't my job. I don't mean to be so clumsy. I wish we could all hit the reverse button on life so they could live the last day over again. I feel like I should hug them but I don't know them. There is a pause as silent cries distort their faces. I don't know what else to say. Opal is there, she takes the teenager's hand but the girl pulls it away and turns to the mother. They cry and hold each other. There is no room in their grief for us. Opal walks them to the chapel while I turn and walk back to the desk where I have to do the paperwork. We were too late. Working in an emergency room is like the proverbial barn door and stolen horse. I don't want to do this anymore. I want to prevent things from getting this far. Maybe I'll become a shrink.

I type the emergency room record since my handwriting is totally illegible. I feel some nausea. I never managed to become immune to death. It always affects me. One of the cops sticks his head into the office: "You win a few, you lose a few, and some get rained out." Policemen have developed an unusual sense of humor for times like this. I'm not offended. I realize his blunt attempt at humor is intended to soften the cold sharpness of self-inflicted death. He wasn't cruel, though some might think of it that way. He was helping to correct the painful imbalance in all of our minds. I thank him and return to my typing. I probably won't sleep tonight even if there aren't any more patients. Even if Monday mornings are quiet times in emergency rooms.

Five years later I'm in Southern California. I'm a shrink—or rather—a psychiatrist. Becoming a headshrinker requires four years of on-the-job training with primitive Indian tribes in the Amazon basin. Becoming a psychiatrist requires three years of specialty training both with the seriously mentally ill and with adult children of normal parents who experience milder forms of mental anguish common to all people. It was no picnic. Of the five physicians who started residency training together, I alone finished on schedule and only one other remained in medicine. But I'm satisfied I am doing what I should do. I don't see as many broken bodies, but I see many more broken minds and warring families. Somehow I feel I can help a little more. I feel I can intervene in lives sooner; I can prevent some disasters.

One particular morning I am in church. Our minister is a marvelous guy. He prepares his sermons for seven hours and it shows. This morning he is drawing on the writings of John Woolman and Carl Jung. I am fascinated. You can hear a pin drop during his delivery. You can also hear the phone ringing in the office. It usually stops after a few rings; most people realize the service is going on and have the courtesy to hang up. But this time the phone continues to ring. Finally Don stops preaching and asks an usher to go answer it. We wait in silence until the usher comes out and says it's for Dr. Hageseth. As I go to answer it, Don offers a prayer. He fears some human tragedy. I'm not so gracious. I'm annoyed.

The voice on the phone is that of an older woman. She is hysterical. Her nineteen year old son has had problems for over a year and they have been getting worse. They have been thinking about getting him in to see me. In fact they have an appointment next week. But he just ran out of the house in frenzied anger without any clothes on. Could I help?

Well, no, I can't. Not now. She needs the police or the help of friends. If they find him, I would be glad to see the young man. Yes, even today, Sunday. But at the moment I can do nothing. I ask her to please call me when they find him. I return to the service and to the sermon.

No calls come that day. The next morning I pick up the paper and read about a young man who committed suicide on Sunday morning about 10:45 by throwing himself in front of a train. He had no clothes on at the time. I put the paper down. The phone call had been precisely at 10:45. Psychiatry does not prevent me from being a day late and a dollar short. If they had only come in the week before. Even though I didn't have to confront the family directly, I still had my own sense of tragedy to deal with. I still felt the icy coldness of self-inflicted death. I still felt like an impotent observer. How to cope? How to carry on as if nothing affected me?

Though I am a psychiatrist, death still shadows me. Stories of abuse still haunt my sleep. I try to be detached and clinical, but underneath I still wonder if I'm cut out for this sort of thing. I am coming to understand why the psychiatrists I disliked in medical school were so cool. It was their defense. But there must be a better defense than distance. There must be a better way to deal with human suffering than becoming analytical and intellectual. There must be a way to stay involved with people and retain warmth and compassion without going under yourself.

My four year old son walks into the kitchen wearing my sport coat and carrying my briefcase. He has my stethoscope around his neck. He bends over and pretends to listen to the dog's heartbeat. He looks up at me and grins and then offers me a turn with the stethoscope. I smile and then I laugh. And we laugh together. I pick him up and give him a big hug. I love him so much. And in that moment I feel some release from the tragedy. I guess it's time to get to work. I realize to survive and to love, I must seek out the moments of beauty and play. I must pay attention to them. If I overlook them, I will surely go down with the depressions that surround me.

A couple more years pass. I'm finally living in Colorado. Seeking the positive, seeking an end run about human adversity, I read *The Road Less Travelled* (by M. Scott Peck,

1978, Simon & Schuster). I am looking for other perspectives on life. Psychology doesn't help with the ultimate questions. In fact it often labels those who look for such answers—especially those who find them—as neurotic. I want to throw myself into the optimistic side of life. I would like to be upbeat and let the world's misery take care of itself. I go to visit Scott Peck, and, surprised, I return with his manuscript, *People of the Lie* (M. Scott Peck, 1983, Simon & Schuster). Just when I think I can lose myself in some optimistic psycho/spiritual detachment, I find myself looking for the devil. Scotty found he couldn't look at love and growth without considering the problem of human evil. I didn't have to look far, no farther than my consulting room.

I had been seeing Doris for over a year. She was starting to look like a multiple personality. I saw her change in front of my eyes. Even her children said, "Mom is like different people. When she's nice, she's really nice. And when she's not, she's really scary." I always identify strongly with the children of mentally ill or alcoholic parents.

One personality was virtually demonic. Her face contorted and her voice changed. Her eyes narrowed and became hooded and reptilian. She laughed with a surreal voice and made fun of me. She spoke of Doris in the third person and how one day she would kill her and "you won't be able to stop it." I inquired when this personality first became part of Doris and with a sneer, it told me its story.

"When she was five Doris went off to Bible school. You know her mom was home in bed, drunk as usual. Mom was always in bed, 'sick' with this or that. She just laid there and played her religious music; sometimes the same record all day long, over and over. Well, Smart-Ass Doctor, Doris was given a picture of Jesus that day. She was told to take it home and put it on her bedroom wall. Then, that night she was supposed to have her parents come in and kneel with her as she knelt and prayed for Jesus to come into her heart. Well, Mommy was too sick, but Daddy was there. He was a deacon in the church. Doris had on her little sheer nightie. She kneeled down and as she began to pray for Jesus to enter her heart, Daddy leaned over her and his weight pushed down on her. She was overshadowed by him, you could say. He started making movements with his body that she didn't understand but somehow she knew were very, very naughty. Like he wanted to enter Doris' heart. If Daddy was Jesus' friend, Doris wasn't. Doris was bad. Doris was evil. And so Doris prayed that whatever else was out there should come to her aid. That's when I came. I gave her comfort for a while. I gave her friendship in her loneliness. And when I choose to, I will take her home. But a lot of men and a lot of Christians are going to pay...and pay...and pay. And that includes you, Dr. Christian."

Her story isn't over yet. I can only say that therapy with excellent people (experts other than myself) and even an exorcism by loving clergy haven't solved the problem. Not Yet.

As Doris and her therapists struggle with evil, so must all persons who live a life of personal awareness. While looking for love, optimism, and growth, you will also discover pain and evil. An understanding of humor must take human adversity (in all its forms) into account or it will be trivial. Life isn't merely difficult, it is *exceedingly difficult*. Pain and illness and abuse and evil exist. What balances out all the adversity? How do people survive? How do they grow? How do they create? Through humor you say? It would be nice if it were that simple, but no, not simply humor, in and of itself. No. Love is what really balances out the adversity and ultimately overcomes it. And one wonderful way love can be expressed is via positive humor. When humor is positive, it helps us cope and it helps us grow. It helps us express our love. It helps us create, and in special moments, it helps us procreate. Positive humor can help shift human consciousness to healing, to love, and to peacemaking.

The same day Doris told me of her rape and of her dark companion, I received a most unusual call. One which I now believe wasn't a mere coincidence. Jane Boulter, the director of education at our local hospital, wanted to clarify my role in an upcoming workshop on "Health and Humor." C.W. Metcalf, a local actor, mime and communications consultant had started the process with her. He would be the funny guy, I would be the straight man. He would present the humor, I would teach the health. Thanks a lot, that's like being asked to be the hygiene teacher in a junior high school. But what the heck. Sure, I'd do it.

Our first day-long presentation was a huge success. I talked about the body/mind relationship and Norman Cousins. C.W. taught some mime. Other nearby hospitals wanted workshops for their staffs. With each succeeding workshop, we began to teach each other what we knew intuitively and what we had learned through study. We synthesized a greater understanding of the subject. When we went to other communities, our material expanded in response to audience need. The feedback from our participants shaped our understanding. Within a year we were going coast-to-coast.

And so my patients and my audiences began to teach me about positive humor. I lectured, I performed the therapy, and in return I learned from the lives and responses of others. Their reactions to the workshop material and their stories taught me about humor in a way that no book or comedian ever could. Many were living successful lives in spite of stress and adversity. Their examples served to teach me what is funny and how and when to use humor positively—be it in the face of illness or following the death of a loved one, be it in business or in simple problems of everyday friendships, be it in marriage or in raising children. They had incorporated humor into their lives. They knew humor was essential to their survival and success.

I had spent a long time learning about the pain of life. I had learned about illness, death, and evil. Now I would allow myself to learn how the clown within all of us—our childlike, playful clown—helps us survive and helps us live more lovingly.

CHAPTER IV

More Than Jokes

The Three Pathways to Humor

Y ou're the joke doctor. You're supposed to be very funny, so tell me a joke. I can't remember jokes, so I must not have a sense of humor. My cousin is very funny; he knows a lot of jokes. This guy I work with knows lots of jokes and not one of them is clean; I wish he didn't have a sense of humor.

Jokes equal humor, right? If you want to be funny, if you want to improve your sense of humor, go to the local Comedy Store and learn some jokes. Write down some jokes, or at least the punch lines, then you will have a sense of humor. Right? Not exactly.

An essential first lesson about positive humor teaches that jokes are not the primary pathway to mirth. Every time I am in front of an audience, I ask the following question: How many of you remember and tell jokes well? Two percent raise their hands. Then I ask: How many of you believe you have a reasonably good sense of humor? Ninety five percent or more raise their hands. Why this difference in perception? In the common mind, the concept of a "sense of humor" is much broader than merely telling jokes. As I watch what people laugh at, as I listen to their stories, I find three pathways into the humor center of the human heart.

The object of this chapter is to describe the three methods of stimulating humor and convince you that you may increase your sense of humor without learning a single joke. Don't get me wrong; jokes are a lot of fun. I just want to make very clear from the outset that their role is not the central one most people presume.

HURT YOUR FACE
(Non verbal interactive humor)

How old were you when you had your first humor experience? When I ask this question of an audience, I get silence. Most people think it might be a trick question. They are embarrassed to guess for fear that they might be way off. Some people venture four years of age, others guess two. A few bold souls suggest it occurs during infancy. This is not a simple question. Many psychologists believe humor to be a function of language and a process involving abstract thought.

I believe humor first expresses itself in the smiling response, at about eight weeks of age. As a parent holds an infant, each makes eye contact, and then both minds become conscious of one another at the same time. Each face communicates the delight of the surprise. Reciprocal smiling is the first interactive recognition of the consciousness of another person. It conveys delight and greeting. "Hello, little one, welcome to the world." Creation itself is celebrated in the moment by both parent and infant. What happens over the next months? The parent and infant spend long periods of time looking into one another's eyes, smiling and laughing. At times, the laughter may be quite robust. The parent may play with all sorts of facial expressions to elicit more laughter. Even the chairman of the board may become an absolute fool as he tries to get his grandchild to laugh with him. I ask the parents in the audience, "How many of you believe that your child had a sense of humor by four months of age?" Eighty five percent raise their hands. The other fifteen percent aren't so sure. Nobody denies that her infant experienced humor during infancy.

Now, how do you get a baby to laugh? Tell it a joke? Oh, sure, "Pat and Mike went down to the river, Pat fell in..." By the time you get that far, the kid is playing with your glasses or blowing bubbles. Do you suggest something off color to stimulate the child to think about some forbidden subject? No way, the child has not learned of the forbiddens. Not yet. To stimulate the infant's sense of humor you make eye contact and play with your face. You grin like a clown, you blow bubbles, you puff your face up, you even use your hands to distort your face. Anything to get that gleeful laughter response. Those moments of shared laughter between the parent and infant are the high point of the parenting experience. It's all downhill after that.

The ability of the human face to stimulate laughter continues throughout life. Even into senility. It is the first method of stimulating humor to be acquired in growth and development. And interestingly, it is the last to disappear in senescence. Nursing home personnel know that fact. Those who don't burn out, the ones who continue to care for the aging, are characterized by a willingness to approach the old folks, make eye contact, and smile broadly right in their faces. The residents may not understand what is going on verbally or abstractly, but they smile and laugh in response. In their minds, it *is* a humor experience.

A mime is a wonderful example of how non verbal behavior can stimulate laughter, how body movements and the use of facial expression can communicate better than words. What does a mime do to his face to enhance it's expression? He puts on "white face" that allows the highlighting of the eyes, eyebrows, and mouth. All of those components that convey meaning in a smile.

By the way, do you know why the Mona Lisa is such an enigmatic painting? Why her smile is so hard to figure out? The Mona Lisa has no eyebrows. Eyebrows help convey the expression of the face. Women with light eyebrows almost always darken them. Darkened eyebrows aren't merely aesthetic, they allow facial expression to be more clear. Whenever eyebrows are penciled in, they take a rounded shape that is suggestive of a bright or cheerful expression. Never a frown. We men with light eyebrows may be misinterpreted from time to time because of the ambivalence our face conveys when our eyebrows fail to express our intention very clearly. When I am playing with my face on stage, I always take my glasses off and emphasize my expressions with my multiwrinkled forehead.

To demonstrate how humor is stimulated by the face, I ask my audiences to stand, take a deep breath, and give me the biggest smiles they've got. I tell them to smile like Mary Lou Retton, our olympic gymnast who showed every molar in the process of her smile. In fact, I suggest they smile so hard they hurt their faces.

Which reminds me of an experience in medical school. Whenever I say "hurt your face," I remember being on obstetrics, watching babies being born. I helped a bit and after a while, I delivered a few myself. One night I was up chatting with the nurses. One of the older women had eight children of her own besides having delivered a couple hundred babies over the years. I asked her what it felt like to deliver a baby, since being male, I would never really know. She told me to put my index and middle fingers in my mouth at both corners. "There now, pull your lips out and stretch them over your head." I got the idea.

Anyway, I invite people to stand, breathe, and smile. Big clown smiles. Not the corporate-board-of-director smile or the I'm-too-important-to-look-foolish smile. No macho smiles either; they aren't smiles, they look more like death threats. I encourage the non-believers—especially the non-believers—to give it their best shot, just this once. They stand, they breathe, (and reluctant or not) they smile—and they laugh. They sit down and they continue to laugh. Finally their brain says to their face, "What's so funny, dummy?" And, a little embarrassed with themselves, they wipe the smile off. But while they smiled they were feeling happy. They were laughing and enjoying humor even though nobody had told a joke.

Then I go a step further. Stand, breathe, smile,....Hold the smile, let the breath out. Now turn and look at the person next to you. Make eye contact. This time, the room explodes into laughter. It often takes two minutes or more before they quiet down. Why? No jokes were told, yet the whole room is laughing.

38

(This has worked with every audience, including Marine Corps Generals.) When conscious eye contact is made and the setting is appropriate, the smiling human face elicits our most primitive and yet elegant humor experience. It recalls our first humor experience and all the security and love we felt at the time. Neglect during infancy cripples a child psychologically for the rest of life. The absence of a smiling, consistent caretaker constitutes neglect.

In this process, people often are not sure of what I am getting at. You mean I should make funny faces all the time? No, I am not suggesting you walk down the street with a clown face. That is a good way to get a seventy-two hour examination at the local psych unit. Or at least it will provide you an introduction to some very interesting people. Setting must be accounted for when choosing to play with your face.

The exchange of delight and laughter *is* a humor experience. Humor's first function in life is to convey love and security. Humor isn't just so much fluff; it is absolutely essential to human survival. It is one of the principle ways that love is expressed. Think about it. How can you convince your infant you love her? You can change her diapers, you can feed her, you can hold her, you can speak to her, and *you can smile at her and laugh with her*. I have often suspected a divine hand in the process. When an infant is first born, her pooh-pooh doesn't smell. Her bottom is sweet to look at and sweet to smell. Her parents delight in her bottom. Just when the stuff "down there" begins to smell, something starts going on at the other end of the kid that attracts them. There is a smiling face up there. Something to distract them from the unpleasant smell of the substance that is beginning to resemble its adult counterpart.

To change your humor experience you must be prepared to let your face play. In fact, you must be willing to take risks not only with your facial expression, but your whole body as well. When we get to gelastolalia and the zygomaticus progression, this will become clearer. Stay with me.... soon we'll be speaking the same language.

A TWELVE INCH PIANIST
(The use of forbidden subjects to stimulate humor)

The second principle way humor is elicited is by inviting a person to think about a subject that, by its nature, is forbidden, off-color, dirty, tasteless, irreverent, etc. Just as the non-verbal interactive method has its origin in early development during infancy, the debut of forbiddens occurs around the "terrible two's." When else?

Imagine you're two years of age. Your language skills aren't much. You know a few nouns, a few verbs, and on a good day you can put several words together in a meaningful sentence. You are beginning to say "no" to the giants in your life, the ones you call "Mommy and Daddy." Lots of things don't work out the way you would like and that upsets you. Mommy and Daddy no longer just hold you and smile, they expect you to learn complex concepts and behaviors. For example, they expect you to understand that you have a gastrointestinal tract and demand you manage it. At the ripe old age of two years they expect you to know there are sophisticated neural sensors at the distal end of the gastrointestinal tract that sense fullness, consistency, and pressure. You grasp this idea with difficulty, but sense it is important. They are going to judge your value as a human being on how well you manage the products of your gastrointestinal tract—how well you interpret the sensors' input and behave with respect to that information. If it is moderately full and solid, you can wait. If it is liquid, you can interrupt anything and cry the magic word, "potty." If it is gas, you are to modulate the tension of the muscles at the distal end of the gastrointestinal tract to allow the pressure to diminish without the accompaniment of sound.

Just when you think you have it fully understood, Uncle Enoch comes to visit. He is getting older and is a little "hard of hearing." He makes that forbidden sound, you laugh, the grown ups frown, and then they send the dog out of the room. Adults say the "twos" are terrible. Well, they are no picnic for the kid going through them either.

The growing child is constantly testing the limits of the forbiddens. He is constantly looking for what will be greeted with a chuckle or a frown. He is deciding on his own set of forbiddens. A very compliant child doesn't squabble much about them. A more difficult child tests the boundaries every day. Finally, the cutting-edge of the matter appears around five years of age. It relates to a normal physiological function of every human body having to do with cleaning the upper airway of dust particles before the air is inhaled into the lungs. Little hairs and mucus clean the air as it passes through the nose. The substance of the subject is "buggars." Many parents have strong reactions to this subject, as if it were as potentially profane as substances relating to the other end. Six year old boys know the difference between broccoli and buggars. They won't eat their broccoli.

Whenever a person is allowed to think of some forbidden subject, it elicits a humor response. When two persons cross a forbidden line together and are conscious of "getting by with it," they share a humor experience. And the humor is amplified by that sharing.

Stimulating forbiddens is one of the principle methods of eliciting humor. Many performers, especially stand up comics, use this method. Since free speech came along, many comedians have expended their energies attempting to find new ways to surprise you with "the F word." Other forbidden subjects include Ethiopian jokes, ethnic humor that portrays a race or nationality as stupid, slow, or sub-human, or so-called "black humor" such as dead baby jokes or what to do with a dead cat. Numerous books have been published which regale the reader with a never-ending supply of tasteless jokes and forbidden humor. For my purposes here, I will content myself with anatomical forbiddens and occasional forays into well-meaning and good natured blasphemy. (Not blasphemy exactly, just taking pokes at religious subjects which on first hearing, sound forbidden—though every minister, priest, or rabbi has a full supply of such quips.)

A note is in order regarding courtesy. Stretching courtesy or making fun of pointless rituals may be a jolly lot of fun.

But it can be overdone. The use of the forbidden pathway in humor is often a matter of degree. It should be possible to enjoy plenty of satirical play with rituals without being frankly disagreeable or consistently discourteous.

When children are severely punished to enforce the forbiddens, they become what psychiatrists describe as "anal retentive" personalities. On the street, they are called "tight asses." They are scrupulously clean, fold their dirty laundry before putting it in the hamper, and have very muted senses of humor.

We judge other people by what forbiddens they allow in humor propagation. Those people who allow more forbiddens than we do are gross, dirty, or immoral. Those who allow fewer forbiddens than we do are up-tight or puritanical. Those who share our level of forbiddens are people we consider to be very funny—people who, we think, have a very good sense of humor.

For many people, there are times when hard-core words convey humor better than any common word could. Consider how the hard-core word in the following story conveys humor better than any common word could.

Helga and Herman had been married fifty-six years. They were in their eighties. Herman was getting ready to die. Looking forward to it, he was awaiting a sign from God. He had heard about the bright light you see when you enter the death experience. One night he had been up for awhile and came to the bed and shook Helga.

"Wake up, Helga. I just had a sign from God. I think I'm going to die soon." He was excited, not afraid. He was ready to go.

"For Pete's sake, Herman, what is it this time?"

"Helga, it was a sign from God. I was up going to the bathroom."

"Herman, that's no sign from God, you've been doing it for years. I think you need your prostate fixed."

"No, Helga, this was different. I went in to the bathroom. It was dark. I lifted the lid, just like you told me. And as I did, the room was filled with a beautiful blue-white light. I put the lid down and the light went out. I lifted it up and it came back on. Helga, it was a miracle."

"Herman, will you get back to bed? You got your head crooked on your neck and you've been pissing in the refrigerator again."

Somehow that story just wouldn't work if you had to use the word "urinate" instead of "the P word."

The use of hard core words generally functions to distinguish subcultures in our pleuralistic society, particularly racial and religious sub-groupings. Every group has its forbiddens. We respect the boundaries of our particular subculture, while we often look upon the forbiddens of another subculture with some dismay; either they are too up-tight or too loose. Some subjects, including body functions, anatomy, sexuality, religion, or politics, are subjects for humorous interchange throughout the culture, but how they are expressed or alluded to varies widely. Where a North Dakota farmer might allude to premarital sex by saying the couple had "a roll in the hay", an inner city laborer might say they "f____ their brains out." Within one's own subculture the phrase is accepted and appropriate; outside one's subculture the words are banal or offensive.

An example of a religious forbidden includes stories where God is spoken of colloquially or in an informal way to convey the action. The following describes a phone call that the Pope received recently. It was a collect call from God. The Pope was pretty excited, after all, it's not everyday you hear directly from God, even when you are the Pope.

"Pope John Paul, this is God. How are you doing?"

"Well, God,...Wonderful. It's so good to hear from you. Why are you calling me? I mean....God, it's been so long..."

"John Paul, I have some good news and some news you may not want to hear."

"God, what's the good news?"

"Well, two years from this very moment...the whole world will be united into one church. All divisions will cease."

The Pope was overcome. He was nearly in tears, "God, what could possibly be bad news? I have worked for this moment all my life. What could possibly be bad?"

"John Paul, I don't know how to break this to you, but I'm calling collect from Salt Lake City."

Old motifs may be used with a twist when a forbidden concept is surprisingly introduced. The unsuspected punch line is amplified when it suggests a forbidden word, even though the word isn't actually spoken, as in the following example.

A man walked into a bar with a brief case under his arm. Though he appeared very wealthy (having driven up in a Ferrari), he also appeared very depressed. He ordered a double. Then he placed his brief case on the bar and opened it. A little man dressed in a tuxedo climbed out. Then the sad looking man took a small piano out and placed it on the bar. The little man seated himself on a little piano stool and started to play. He was excellent. He played classics, jazz, anything. The bartender stared in amazement.

"Hey, buddy, I've never seen anything like that. Where did you ever find him?"

The depressed man wasn't very enthusiastic. "Well, it's like this. I was marooned on a desert island and about to die. I was digging in the sand for water when I happened upon this vase. I brushed the sand off and a genie appeared. She said I had rescued her from her prison and she would grant me any three wishes.

"Well, my first wish was to be rescued, and, as you can see, I'm here and I'm safe. Second, I asked for money, lots of it. And you can see I am very wealthy. But then, in my haste—or maybe the genie didn't hear me right—I made my third request. And now I'm stuck with this twelve inch pianist."

By now you probably have the idea. Sure, there is surprise as an element in these examples, but the real punch is in the fact that some forbidden subject is admitted into consciousness. To employ this form of humor, you need to decide on what forbidden subjects and words are acceptable to you. More importantly, when you use this form of humor, you need to be sensitive to what is acceptable to your listeners. Finally, pay attention to the setting; it will determine when forbiddens may be used or should be avoided.

WHEN A W.C. IS NOT A WATER CLOSET
(The use of jokes, plays on words, absurdities. Verbal humor.)

The third way of eliciting humor is what most people imagine when they first think of humor. This is why, when people first meet me, they expect to encounter a psychiatric joke repository. In the common mind, joking equals humor. This pathway depends on verbal skills, double meanings, and surprise. Children gradually develop this skill from age four through the teens. At first the double meanings are so clumsy that adults simply can't see the jokes as funny. Have you ever tried to listen to the humor of a four year old? It doesn't do much for a grown-up mind, yet the kids think themselves to be marvelously funny. Older grade-school children succeed, on occasion, in sharing a joke with parents. They are beginning to get the idea of pacing the joke and hitting the punch line appropriately. Later on, jokes may be shared between adults and teenagers because they have greater life experience and language ability. Unfortunately, the need for separation usually demands that teenagers avoid including adults, especially their own parents, in their joking experiences. But in those cases where parents and teenagers do succeed in sharing jokes, it provides healthy and loving experiences for both. It beats tough love by a long shot.

Playing with words can produce accidental moments of humor. More often, however, if we want to be funny, we rely on jokes passed from person to person. *Hence plagiarism is absolutely essential to the process.* In academia, plagiarism is a capital crime. In humor, it is the lifeblood of the whole process. Can you imagine always having to cite who first told a given joke? That would kill a lot of good joking. Whole comedy routines are a different matter.* That's a matter of performance and copyright. But jokes are meant to be traded, modified to your own use, and passed on. After all, it would be virtually impossible to really find the origin of a given joke. If you want to tell

---

* *Certain terms used in this book and my audio tape series have been tradmarked by C.W. Metcalf and company; they include the Zygomaticus Progression, Stand, Breathe & Smile, Humor Inventory, 4 Face Fotos, and Humor Support Groups.*

jokes, freely steal them, adapt them to your persona, and let 'em rip.

I received this following story from a Dominican priest. It provides an illustration of how jokes are constructed. Notice there is a gentle use of forbiddens along the way.

"W.C"

An English lady, while visiting Switzerland, was looking for a room and asked a local schoolmaster if he could recommend one. He took her to several rooms, and when everything was settled, she returned home to make final arrangements for moving. When she arrived home, the thought occurred to her that she had not seen a W.C. (water closet or bathroom) around the place. She immediately wrote to the schoolmaster asking him where the W.C was. The schoolmaster didn't know the meaning of "W.C.," so with a priest's assistance, he came to the conclusion that it meant Wayside Chapel (a small building beside the road where travellers could rest or pray). He sent a letter back to the English lady, which read as follows:

Dear Madam:

I take great pleasure in informing you that the nearest W.C. is situated only nine miles from the house in a beautiful grove of trees. It is capable of holding 32 people. It is open only on Mondays and Thursdays.

There are a great number of people expected during the summer months, so I would suggest that you come early, although there is usually plenty of standing room. This is an unfortunate situation, especially if you are in the habit of going regularly.

You will, no doubt, be glad to hear that a number of people bring their lunch and make a day of it, while others who can't afford it, arrive just in time. I would recommend Thursdays because, on that day, there is an organ accompanist. The acoustics are excellent and even the slightest sound can be heard anywhere.

It may interest you to know that my daughter met her husband in the W.C., and they were married there. I can still vividly remember the rush for seats. Seven people crowded into seats for four. It was wonderful to see the expressions on their faces.

Unfortunately, my wife is rather delicate, so she has not attended in over a year. Naturally, it pains her very much—not to be able to go more often. I shall be delighted to reserve a seat for you if you wish, where you can be seen by all. Hoping to be of assistance, I am, Sincerely Yours,

I hope that gives you the idea. Dissecting jokes is like dissecting frogs. You understand how they work, but it kills them in the process.

The double meaning is established early between water closet and wayside chapel. Then with each sentence another surprise comes and with it, a humor stimulus.

WITH THREE YOU GET EGGROLL
(Combination of the three components for optimal effect.)

In my experience, truly funny people use a combination of the three humor forms. Their faces animate the story, or sometimes they deadpan with their faces in order to provide a surprising contrast. The content often has some mildly forbidden theme. Finally, the joke cracks with surprise as the unexpected juxtaposition of meanings becomes clear.

Experiment with the "W.C." passage. Read it out loud to some friends, your family, or co-workers. Take time as you read it. Let the chuckles build between the punch lines. Make eye contact with your listeners as you read and allow yourself to smile or giggle if you are so inclined. See whether you can be aware of the non-verbal interactive component with your listeners while reading this humorous passage sprinkled with gentle forbidden themes.

CHAPTER V

A Deeper Look

The Broad Definition of
Positive Humor

Now that the pathways to eliciting a humor response are cleared, we need to examine the broad concept of "a sense of humor." It's time to tack down and flesh out the concept. Get to the heart of the matter. Take the bull by the tail and look the issue squarely in the face.

Corny metaphors, like cliches, shouldn't be touched with a ten foot Pole—or a six foot Norwegian for that matter. Such metaphors are like generalizations, which we know are always false.

The early reformers of the Christian Church argued over faith and works. The Protestants said faith was the whole nine yards; it alone could do the job. Works would logically come from faith, but effort need only be directed towards faith. The Catholics held that doing good works alone would lead to faith. Merely doing good works was enough since faith would naturally follow.

Twentieth century psychologists, our modern day secular clergy, have the same controversy about psychotherapy. Insight or behavior change? Analyze, analyze, analyze, then insight will follow together with changed feelings. After that, behavior will automatically change. The opposing view of the behaviorists holds that behavior change *per se* will result in new feedback from the environment. And they argue this new feedback will lead to new feelings about the self.

As in so many controversies, both positions are true to an extent. But what does this have to do with humor? When we approach the concept of humor, we need to realize that a sense of humor is comprised of two elements: A perspective—a way of perceiving the world—and behaviors that express that perspective. Humor is not merely the ability to laugh easily or often, although it often involves smiling and laughter. Nor is humor a way of looking at the world that provides for private amusement, a mental exercise kept within the cerebrum. Though humor may be experienced privately, we have already seen that it is principally an interactive process of communication and even love. If a humorous perception isn't expressed via behavior, it is like loving someone and never ever letting on that the love exists. It doesn't do much for either person. After a while, it rots within the heart and becomes bitter and sour. Humor that isn't expressed often suffers the same fate and manifests it's presence as cynicism, satire, or sarcasm.

PERSPECTIVE AND BEHAVIOR

There's a saying on the street: "What you see is what you get." But that's not exactly right. A more accurate statement would go: "What you get is what you are capable of seeing." Perception and behavior go hand in hand. You act on what you perceive, not necessarily what is really out there. And it follows that your behavior often shapes your world. Your behavior determines, at least in part, what you encounter. So we could say your perception is shaped by your behavior. And thus we see a vicious cycle developing. Behavior shapes perception, which shapes behavior, which in turn shapes perception again, and so on. We reinforce our world views through our behavior, and as we do, our personalities become more fixed. Our responses— which we like to think are reasoned and logical—become like knee jerks, automatic and programmed. That is why change is so difficult. What we see, we learn. What we learn, we practice. What we practice, we become. Hence, to understand what comprises a sense of humor, you will have to understand perception and behavior and their interplay. To change your sense of humor, you will have to change your perspective *and* your behavior.

How do you position yourself to look at life? After all, we agree it is not a simple matter, i.e. to change your entire outlook on life. You can, however, look at life from a slightly different angle from time to time. People with a positive sense of humor constantly shift their perspective so they can experience some surprise or absurdity. They play with their perceptions. Then they behave in accordance with their perception and express their humor. They let their amusement become public. They smile, they laugh, they editorialize about their perceptions. They do not keep their ideas to themselves, though in some circumstances the setting may require some temporary suppression. Let me offer some examples from real life to demonstrate the interrelationship of behavior and perception in humor propagation.

In World War II the Allies landed in Sicily on a beach called Anzio. American troops found themselves in tough combat with the German army. Truth be known, the Americans had wished they had been met by the Italians. They had hoped for less fighting and a little more partying. Unfortunately the battle was tough and the casualties numerous. In the first waves of troops landing on the beach was a young physician who had the thankless job of triage. He had to divide the wounded into three groups. There were those whose wounds were so severe they would likely die regardless of the care they were given. Since resources on a battlefront are limited, they were put off to a side where they would likely die. If any lived they would be cared for later. Then there were those with trivial wounds who, with a little first aid, could return to combat immediately. They were patched up and sent back to the battle. Finally, there were those who had serious wounds, so serious that they could not return to fight. But with a little effort they would live. These men were treated in a staging area on the beach. Later they would be returned to a hospital ship and probably home. What the doctor observed has influenced the medical understanding of pain ever since. The men in that middle group were laughing. They were playing pranks on each other. They were cheerful and even telling jokes. For them, the war was over. They were heroes, they were going home, they were alive. For them it was their lucky day. They were playful because they were released from war. The euphoria of release spurred their levity. (I have seen many gunshot wound victims and never have I seen one laugh and never have I heard one proclaim it to be his lucky day.) And what was more striking? They only required ten percent of the morphine predicted by the seriousness of their wounds. They laughed, they had a radically different perspective on their experience, and they didn't feel pain—or if they did, they were not bothered by it. Their use of humor coincided with vastly diminished suffering. Perhaps they were receiving their own internal morphine in the process. An adaptation which is life saving, endorphin release in the brain produces euphoria and relief of pain. Belly laughter triggers endorphin release.

I was invited to present a humor workshop at a lakeside resort in central Texas for a corporate annual meeting. It was typical August weather for those parts: 102 degrees, 95% humidity, a cloudless sky, and not a hint of a breeze. The afternoon was free so everybody was heading out on the water to cool off. As I was crossing the parking lot to my room, a police car, red lights flashing, screeched to a stop in the parking lot. A teenage girl, obviously very upset, blurted out that there was a boating accident, that "it's just terrible." Being a few steps away, I offered that I was a doctor, could I help. (I thought the better of telling him I was a psychiatrist.) He looked relieved to have me along.

We ran down to the dock. There on the back of a pontoon boat was a young man with a severely injured leg. I have seen a lot of badly injured limbs. (I left emergency medicine to avoid this sort of thing.) He had fallen off the front of a boat and it had gone over him. He had enough presence of mind to keep his head down, but in the process his right lower leg was hit by the propeller. Two wounds on his leg exposed both of the bones, broken and jagged. He had an injury that could be termed "filet of leg." He appeared to be in shock, so pale you could see light through his hand; it was just like wax. He was conscious, but in a great deal of pain. He was sweating profusely. I couldn't feel his pulse. I checked the leg; there was no active bleeding. We positioned life jackets around it to provide support, and I asked the bystanders to give us some room; perhaps a couple of them could make us some shade. By that time I was sweating profusely too. We were a long distance from anywhere. Texas is like that, everywhere is a long distance from anywhere else. I had no instruments with which to work. I had nothing but my mind and his. If I were to help him, I would have to offer him a way to change his perception.

There are some medical professionals who are using hypnosis to treat acute burn patients. It appears to make them more comfortable so they need fewer narcotics. And in the process of experiencing less pain, the body responds by diminishing the inflammatory response and thus reduces the amount of tissue loss. During the hypnosis, the patient is invited to remember the famous Uncle Remus story of "Brer Rabbit's Laughing Place." Brer Rabbit was about to be eaten by Brer Bear and Brer Fox when he burst out with peals of laughter just remembering his laughing place. Overcome by curiosity, Brer Bear and Brer Fox took Brer Rabbit on a leash to his laughing place. When they got to a big tree in the forest, Brer Rabbit lost it completely—laughed till he cried. Brer Bear and Brer Fox ran to the tree and peered into a big dark hole on the side of the tree to see what was so funny. Rather than being amused, they were attacked by a swarm of bees. They ran away swatting and yelling and letting go of Brer Rabbit in the process. Brer Rabbit, he just laughed all the more. Brer Bear and Brer Fox hollered their complaint, "Brer Rabbit, you said this was a laughing place." Brer Rabbit, rolling on the ground and drunk with laughter, replied, "I said this was *my* laughing place. And it is. This is the funniest thing I ever did see."

So I knelt beside the young man and offered to help him change his perception of the current situation. He readily agreed.

(People in pain are very agreeable when something is offered that might help.) I suggested he relax. "Your leg is badly injured. We will take care of it. As you relax deeply and let your mind go elsewhere, perhaps you can find a place of laughter, a place where you feel safe and happy. Maybe a place like Brer Rabbit found for his special laughing place." I spoke in a low hypnotic repetitive way. He relaxed and within a couple of minutes he was lying back and smiling slightly. I asked him what was going on.

"Well, sir, I'm in Southern California at a place called Paradise Valley."

"Have you ever been there before?"

"No, Sir." (Polite young man, from Texas, I believe.)

"What's going on?"

"Well, Sir, I'm with a bunch of my friends. We have a rope swing and we are swinging out over the water and jumping in."

"Sounds like you're having fun."

"Yes, sir.

"What else are you doing?"

"We are drinking Corona beer right out of the bottle."

"What else, Mike." (His name was Mike.)

"Well, sir, I met a girl."

"What's her name?"

"Carla."

"What's Carla like?"

"Sir, she's a fox."

"Mike, do you have some designs on Carla?"

Big smile, "Yes, Sir."

We continued on, and a little later, the paramedics arrived. When we took his first blood pressure, it was normal (124/84) while his pulse was a little elevated at 104. When we repositioned his leg, he did show evidence of pain. But on the way to the helicopter he was joking with the president of the corporation. "David, I messed my leg up. I guess you could tell. If you want to get any work out of me in the hospital, you will have to get a PC for my room." David was agreeing. Mike added, "It's got to be an IBM."

I have spoken to Mike since. He recalls the pain became

much worse in the hospital after thy gave him some Demerol. Probably because it broke the trance. The focus of his perception returned to his injury.

Finally, there is the story of Norman Cousins as told in his best selling book *Anatomy of an Illness as Perceived by the Patient.* If you haven't read it, you ought to. His writing pioneered respectability for the medical applications of humor. His thesis is much as follows: If the negative emotions such as fear, anger, rage, envy, sadness, hopelessness can make you ill (does anyone disagree?) then it stands to reason that the positive emotions such as love, positive humor, joy, hope, and peace-of-mind will move you in the direction of good health. Norman Cousins had a life threatening illness for which Western medicine has no cure: Ankylosing spondylitis, a connective tissue disease that cripples a person with pain and deforms the back, is often fatal as it chokes off the nerves exiting the spine. Medication only reduces the symptoms, it doesn't cure the underlying process. He decided to undertake more personal involvement in his recovery. *In cooperation with his physician,* he undertook a number of self-directed treatments. He left the hospital because it is a terrible place to be when you are sick. He limited the number of times that he would allow blood tests. Being a friend of Linus Pauling, he took massive doses of vitamin C. (I often wonder where humor in medicine would be today if he had been a pal of Timothy Leary instead of Linus Pauling.) And he stimulated his humor center by watching movies that amused him. He watched them alone and he watched them with friends and family. He laughed often and well, and in the process found that belly laughter gave him up to four hours of pain-free sleep without medication. He finally recovered and wrote his book. Several years later, he had a heart attack and wrote another best seller, *The Healing Heart.* If Norman keeps getting sick and then writing books, he will have quite a string of best sellers.

All three stories are true. All three demonstrate the use of humor in adversity. The application of humor never denied an injury or an illness, or its severity. I didn't tell Mike to get up and dance, that his leg was fine. Humor should not be used to deny reality. But it should be used to cope with adversity and, if possible, grow through it. In each case, humor was associated with a decrease in the perception of pain. Perhaps in the case of belly laughter, the pain itself was diminished as a result of an endorphin release. (You remember endorphins? Right, small children without parents who live indoors all the time.)

TAKE YOURSELF LIGHTLY...
TAKE YOUR WORK IN LIFE SERIOUSLY

The first and most important element in gaining a humorous perspective is to take yourself lightly. You are not the center of the universe, nor are you its director—that job is already taken and you're not qualified. You must first be able to laugh at yourself. Then you may laugh at others because your laughter will be sympathetic, not cynical. For example, when you choose ethnic humor, it will be about your ethnic group first. I frequently joke about Norwegians; I never joke about Blacks or Hispanic people.

The other component of the humor perspective is taking your work in life seriously—but not confusing that with your career. Your work in life *is not* your career. Positive humor affirms the need to take your work in life seriously. It does not deny reality. And—in reality—there is plenty of work to be done both in your career and your work in life. From time to time your career can be the pits. But, if you confuse your career and your work in life, what happens when you retire? You die. If you don't die physically, at least your spirit dies.

What is your work in life if it is not your career? Your work in life is to give of yourself in three ways. First, extend yourself for the psychological and spiritual growth of those people you can influence. For most, this means family, friends, and co-workers first. Then, after they are cared for, you may extend yourself to Russia and Iran. Don't neglect those close to you as you pursue distant altruistic goals. Some famous people have failed to love their family while they seemed to love the rest of the world. Too often, their disciples followed their example and neglected their loved ones as well. How do you "extend yourself" for others' psychological and spiritual growth? You take time, you give your attention, and you help them with the work or play of their lives. You feel with them—both their joy and sorrow. You offer your spirit for company as they seek to understand the meaning of their life. Or you simply are there, so they are relieved of loneliness.

The second part of your work in life involves making amends. Everybody hurts someone else from time to time—sometimes on purpose, other times by accident. When you become aware of having hurt another, go to that person, apologize, and ask what you can do to make up for it. I once committed an almost unpardonable sin: I failed to show up for a speaking engagement. The woman responsible for my being there called me in distress. An audience of two hundred people awaited me—eighty miles distant and I was to be on stage at that moment. There was no way I could get there in time and the convention schedule had to go on. I apologized, of course. And then I followed up with an open letter of apology to the organization and a promise to speak to their group any time, any place, and for no fee.

The third part of your work in life is to make the world a better place while having lived there a while. This does not have to entail winning a Nobel Prize or curing cancer. It is in the simple gestures of life, in the lives you touch, in the gardens you plant, in the spouse, children, or friends you comfort, in music you share, or in the peace you create in your space, however small. After your three-score-and-ten, the ledger keeper notes your net effect on the world was positive. The world is better off because you were there. You returned Creation's gift with interest.

I once had knee surgery. I was a stranger in the hospital where the procedure was performed. Even though I am a doctor, I had my questions, my fears, my uncertainties. My surgeon was skilled in his craft but brief with his words. (What did we say in med school? You can always tell a surgeon, but you can't tell him much.) The nurses were busy with the more needy patients and the never ending paperwork. Who made my day? Who brought brightness into my grey room? The cleaning lady. Rosa was of Mexican origin; she had little formal education. She had no facade to maintain and she didn't know who I was and could have cared less that I was a psychiatrist. Her career was cleaning lady, mopper of vomit, changer of dirty linens. She ranked near the bottom of the hospital pecking order. Yet in my room she was bringer of cheer, the smiling one. Interested in the fact that we both had boys entering adolescence, we wondered whether they would make it through those years; we wondered whether we would make it through those years. I looked foreword to her visits and the smiling and laughter she brought. I cannot recall her telling me a joke, but her sense of humor scored a ten. Rosa was doing her work in life—all three components—better than anyone else in the hospital. (Actually, I don't know about her amends making, but I am sure she did it well.) Maybe it's easier for people like Rosa, maybe they have an easier time taking themselves lightly. They haven't been seduced into avoiding humor out of self importance. They don't confuse their career with their work in life.

THE ISSUE OF OFFENSE

Taking offense involves two people: Those who give offense and those who take offense. Either way, offense destroys humor. Interestingly, those who give offense are not too hard to deal with; they only affect those they encounter at a given moment. They diminish humor, but in a way they are easy to deal with. Once we identify purposeful offense perpetrators, we label them "jerks"—or if we feel profane and the company allows the use of forbidden language, "a_____."

A more malignant problem involves those who go out of their way to be offended. Their willingness to be offended extends their influence far and wide. You never know if one of those mild mannered offense takers is within earshot, ready to give you "whatfor" because of some sort of prejudice you may express. The easily-offended, the meek, *shall* inherit the earth. They will win it as the proceeds from a law suit. The pursuit of litigation, the desire to go out of one's way to be offended, the never ending cry of "foul" constantly eats away any efforts at humor, however mild and inoffensive they try to be. The intent to take offense threatens humor much more seriously than all the jerks of the world. Have you ever worked with someone who is offended by every personal pronoun you use? Do you notice how easily people are offended while driving down a freeway? Just watch sometime and see how many times you see "the international gesture of good will" flashed by an offended motorist.

Perhaps it goes with taking yourself lightly. You may not win any lawsuits, but you will surely live a longer and happier life if you laugh off your impulse to be offended. Interestingly, if you reduce the number of times you choose to be offended by twenty percent, you will increase the world's humor experience by at least forty percent. It may just be, that in being less defensive, less easily offended, you may be safer and certainly more relaxed. Easy going humor—not naivete—may not just help you feel better, it may protect you from this paranoid world.

CONSTANT WILLINGNESS TO BE SURPRISED

If you don't look for beauty, you won't see it. If you don't seek joy, you won't find it. If you are preoccupied with life's troubles, the humorous surprises of life will pass you by. Expect to be amused. The more often you allow yourself to be surprised, the easier it will be to find amusement where you failed to find it before. And look for humor even in the trivial moments of life—most especially in the trivial moments.

I went to Arizona State University for the World Humor and Irony Meeting (WHIM). My son's friend was a student there and invited me to stay with him. Usually I would decline, but housing was scarce and he lived next to campus. When I arrived, I came to understand the word "messy" in a whole different way. He and his roommate had a big (eighty pound) puppy, a parrot, and a rabbit. All enjoyed the full run of the apartment. But the young men did not own a broom. They said they couldn't afford one. I was given the water bed; my host slept on the sofa. The light was burned out in the bedroom, so when I retired, I made my way over the shifting, undulating surface with some uncertainty. I tried to lie very still and fall off to sleep quickly, but the bed discouraged rest. A sprinkling of crumbs between my body and the bottom sheet distracted my attention. I brushed them aside in the dark, prepared a clean spot, and waited for the wave action to die so I could fall off to sleep. The next morning at breakfast my host reminded me to always keep the door to the bedroom closed. I asked why. He explained that the rabbit liked to use the water bed as his litter box. And I thought out loud, "crumbs..."

The same morning I was walking across the campus. The parking lots were massive; I think all students were required to own a car or they wouldn't be admitted. Little covered scooters with orange flashing lights made their rounds giving tickets to any illegally parked vehicles. They made beeping sounds all the time, some sort of warning, I guess. One came by me beeping. It drove on, but I continued to hear the beeping. I looked around and couldn't see any other scooters. Then I realized the beeping was coming from the top of a nearby tree. As I looked up, a mockingbird flew down and by me going "beep...beep...beep."

POSITIVE PARANOIA

Positive humor requires optimism. Pessimism in humor is expressed as irony, satire, sarcasm, or put-down ethnic humor. While regular paranoia involves a suspicious approach to life that sees evil conspiracies everywhere, positive paranoia is the optimistic extreme of being good natured; it stops just shy of being naive. The concept of positive paranoia is simple, "When in doubt, assume the best about a person because people often move in the direction of your expectations." Before this sounds too much like "goody two shoes," notice the first clause, "When in doubt..." If a person is a jerk or a criminal or truly intends to do you harm, respond appropriately. Naive use of humor in such situations could be disastrous. Apply optimism and positive paranoia when the issue is in doubt. Any teacher, most managers, and many parents know that if you expect positive results from people, they are more likely to happen. And conversely, if you expect the worst from people, that may be exactly what you get.

I was five when I first learned about how people respond to expectations. Growing up in North Dakota in the 40's, many of us were poor, and since we were all in it together, it was no big deal. I was doing a self-designed Montessori project; I was in my back yard sifting sand in a big barrel. For hours on end, I was content to sift sand. My brother, five years older than I, had found a treasure. He had a glass insulator from a telephone pole, and it wasn't even cracked. He polished it and thought it was really special. One day he came to me while I was in the middle of my sand project. He said he was going into the house and for me not to take that hammer over there and break his insulator with it. I promised, and after he went in the house, I obediently went over and picked up the hammer. I remember to this day thinking out loud to myself, "Why am I doing this?....I guess because he expects me to." I smashed the insulator just as he emerged from the back door. Being no dummy, I cried as loud as I could so our mother made it outside before he could hit me. My brother is now a physics professor, for several years the chairman of the department of physics at an eastern university. A couple years ago when our mother passed away, he and I were recalling childhood memories. On the day after the funeral, he asked while we were reminiscing, "Why did you break my insulator?" I replied, "Because you expected me to."

I told this story a few months later while doing a presentation for a telephone company in Wyoming. At the end of the program, a line foreman gave me a new resistor. The following Christmas, I gave it to my brother. He replied, "But it isn't green."

HUMORFEEDBACK—GELASTOLALIA

It's not news to tell you that your mind and body are connected. In fact nearly everyone quotes some statistic about illness being fifty (or is it seventy or is it even eighty) percent psychosomatic. Of course, in the common mind, "psychosomatic" is a four letter word and only applies to other people when talking to your doctor. "My illness is *real, not psychosomatic.*" First of all, psychosomatic illness is real and can kill you; it is neither imaginary nor mere pretense. The concept involves acknowledging that the mind/brain are connected to the whole body through complex interrelationships including the endocrine system, the immune system, and the nervous system. When the mind/brain is in trouble, it will affect the rest of the body and illness may result. That illness can be serious enough to kill you, or it may be merely a vexation, a stress disorder.

Biofeedback seeks to alleviate the effects of stress by directly relaxing the body, not by appealing to cognition or exhortation. Biofeedback suggests that if you monitor—get feedback—moment by moment on a given physiological process, you can alter it and be relieved of symptoms associated with it. Illness can be treated and even be cured. Imagine you have tension headaches. When tense, your thinking may be going something like this: "Things are tough. I must work hard. I don't dare to let up. This is a dog-eat-dog place. And I'm not going to be the dog food. Damn, my head hurts. Maybe some Darvon will help and I can keep on truckin'." Then you get hooked up to a biofeedback machine that reports the muscle tension of the muscles in your forehead. At first the tone reports high tension and a needle reports the same on a dial you can see visually. Then you *will* yourself to relax—you don't try, you don't force—you just *let* yourself relax. The tone drops, the needle goes down. After a while, when you enter this relaxed state of mind, your thinking has changed: "Maybe things aren't so bad. I'll work when I need to and I'll relax when I want to. I guess it's hard here, but it's not all that bad. My forehead does feel so much more comfortable." What changed? Only the muscle tension in the forehead. The mind interpreted that decrease of muscle tension to mean that the world is a safer place and that you are more capable of handling it. The mind affects the body, yes. *And the body affects the mind.* You will your body to relax and your mind follows. In fact, it is very hard to let the mind relax if the body remains tense.

One more example before getting to the idea of humorfeedback. Imagine feeling reasonably neutral. Then start making a fist with your dominant hand. Tighten your jaw and narrow your eyes. Start methodically striking your closed fist into the other hand. Breathe short breaths. Continue the process for a minute. What happens? You begin to feel angry. Given some time, you will know who you are angry at and why—and what you might like to do to them. By going through the physical manifestations of anger, you can start experiencing the feeling of anger. You can escalate your previously neutral mood into anger. When dealing with violent patients, our first interventions are directed at relaxing tight muscles, fists etc. We don't tell them to "chill out" or "get mellow." We know that relaxing the physical body will feedback to the mind and bring about the desired result naturally.

So now we get to gelastolalia. Don't bother looking the word up; it's not in the dictionary. I made it up. But it comes from respectable Greek roots and so I proclaim it's birth. You saw it first, right here. It means "Give voice to your laughter." If something strikes you funny, let yourself go. Laugh generously. You will experience a form of biofeedback. Your mind will feel safer and happier. Your sense of humor will improve. It is simple behavioral psychology. The more willing you are to express laughter physically, the more funny something will strike you, and the better sense of humor you will develop.

You are always modifying your humor expression. This concept suggests you modify it in the direction of loosening up and laughing. Normally, in adult life, the opposite is the case. In Chapter IX you will learn about the zygomaticus progression. That will provide an actual step-by-step process for engaging your humor expression more easily.

SO....

Now you should understand the broad concept of a "sense of humor." You know specific information about per-spective and behavior that is practical and applicable. If you want to start changing today, you have some tools. Pick out one topic in this chapter each day and examine how you deal with the concept in a number of different situations. Here are some examples you might try:

1.) If you find you are easily offended, experiment with the opposite. Try to avoid being easily offended and observe the effects of your new behavior on the people who previously "bugged" you. Do they change? Do they seem easier to get along with?

2.) Check out how positive paranoia works. Surely there are situations in your life which are in doubt—individuals who will respond to your expectations. Try assuming the best about them. How do they respond?

3.) Play with your awareness of life. Spend an hour walking on a street or in a park—either alone or with a friendly conspirator. How many potential humorous situations can you see? Count them. You should be able to find five an hour. Hint: In the city, look for pigeons or watch people who are in a hurry.

4.) Play with your self importance. Visit a museum of natural history and notice how long you have been on this Earth. Who will remember you one hundred years from today? What good will it do if they do remember you? Try imagining five billion ink dots spaced one inch apart on a giant piece of paper a few miles big in each dimension. Which dot are you? And remember, you—like all human beings—are biodegradable.

5.) Read the chapter over and make up an exercise of your own. It either needs to apply to your perspective or your behavior—some new idea which you haven't tried before.

Don't expect to succeed with your humor efforts a hundred per cent of the time. If these exercises work one out of three times, that is good enough for a starter. Changes need be applied consciously for six weeks before the new perception/behavior becomes automatic. It takes that long to break old habits and establish new ones.

CHAPTER VI

Who's To Blame?

The Theoretical Basis of Positive vs.
Negative Humor

The next task is to understand how humor relates to adversity and how that understanding distinguishes positive humor from negative humor. While positive humor promotes your growth and that of your loved ones, negative humor promotes or continues human suffering. Clearly humor helps you cope with adversity—all kinds of adversity, regardless of origin. But, the ultimate result of humor may be positive or negative depending on the degree of personal responsibility you bear for the adversity.

I often get angry with psychological therapists, whether they be psychiatrists, psychologists, or social workers, who won't admit they have deep biases. They claim their orientation is valid and even scientific. I once sat in an audience while a psychologist proclaimed the following:

"You are completely responsible for whatever happens to you in life. You bring on all of your own adversity. If you get cancer, you chose it. If you get depressed, you brought it on. If you lose your job, you caused it. You are responsible for your life. Nobody else is. Don't blame anyone else for your own hang-ups. They are your own doing."

Only a month earlier I had attended a conference with a

completely different slant on the idea of responsibility. A panel suggested that life is determined for you. Society, your parents, your siblings, and your family history determine your life down to the last detail. Very few people have much latitude of free choice. In fact, they doubted whether there was any such thing as free choice and hence personal responsibility.

The truth lies somewhere between those extremes. Some adversity comes almost randomly; you have no responsibility for it. It's just a matter of luck. Some adversity is specifically a result of your own actions. You bear full responsibility for it.

I queried the first psychologist about manic depressive disease, which is genetic. He answered me with a quip that was clever and it amused the audience. But he did not answer my question. I then asked him about children who were sexually abused at the age of four; I refuse to see them as responsible for that adversity. He said he didn't know, but wondered if they weren't working out some karma from a past life. I asked, quite seriously, whether he was Hindu. He laughed and went on to someone else's question. It was his show, and he knew how to manage his audience. He knew how to use humor to avoid an issue. He was clever and his humor was negative. His humor denied the validity of my question. His response implied that adversity comes to everyone by his purposeful choice. The audience was denied the knowledge implicit in a thoughtful answer to my questions.

I once consulted on a middle aged man with lung cancer. As I entered his room, he was on the edge of the bed smoking and looking at the floor. He was emaciated; his cancer was advanced. In the course of our conversation I learned he was forty-three and had been smoking three packs a day for thirty years. Numerous times he had been advised to stop or at least cut down, but he didn't. Now, as he was dying, he said he understood his death. He looked at me with a half-smile, laughed slightly, and said, "It's God's will." With this effort at humor, he avoided his responsibility by putting it on God. I have seen that frequently—blaming God for problems a person brings on himself. For the two of us, his humor wasn't particularly negative. But when he shared this idea with his grandchildren, it became negative. He denied his responsibility and with his laughter, unconsciously invited them to follow suit. After all, his suffering was God's will, not a result of his own neglect.

That patient was not unusual. Often, when people ought to accept responsibility for their adversity, they do not. They blame other people, they call it luck, or they implicate God. And then other times, I see the opposite extreme as people grapple with guilt trying to assume responsibility for something altogether out of their hands—something for which they bear no legitimate responsibility.

Figure 1 illustrates how some adverse life events are completely out of our control. However we bear varying amounts of responsibility for the vast majority of adversity that occurs in our life. And we bear *full* responsibility for only a few events.

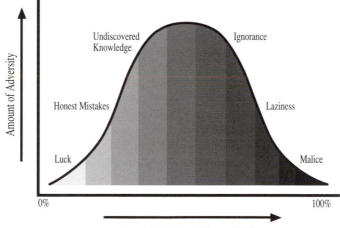

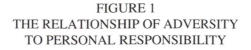

FIGURE 1
THE RELATIONSHIP OF ADVERSITY
TO PERSONAL RESPONSIBILITY

Obviously the issue of personal responsibility has plagued philosophers and psychologists for ages. I don't intend to settle the question in this discussion. I do ask that you accept the proposition that we bear varying amounts of responsibility for the bad things that happen in our lives. It has an important theoretical implication for the positive and negative effects of humor.

Humor used in the face of adversity which has descended upon us—and is not as a result of our own doing—is positive. It helps us cope, survive, and grow. It sustains us while we try to find our way out.

Humor used in the face of adversity which comes to us as a result of our own wrongdoing is defensive. Such humor deflects responsibility, denies culpability, and is used unfairly to project blame elsewhere. The effect of such humor is negative since it sustains suffering and it prevents change in the underlying source of the adversity.

Figure 2 illustrates that relationship. Humor should be avoided when we are responsible for the adversity—even if it helps us escape; for the escape merely prolongs the adversity for ourself or our community. Conversely, humor should be embraced when we are not responsible for our adversity. And it is reasonable to expect a mix in between. It is not an all-or-none proposition. Of course, we do not always understand the source of our adversity, but this illustration provides a rationale for the existential distinction between positive and negative humor. Some examples should clarify this concept.

EXAMPLES

Movies during the first sixty years of the twentieth century portrayed black people as dull, slow, lazy characters who were very funny to *laugh at*. It was thought to be innocent enough by many people, both white and black. But that was before we were conscious of white racism in its many subtle and varied forms. The civil rights movement clarified that such humor reinforced malicious and purposeful bigotry. The humor wiped away the appropriate guilt that white audiences should have felt.

68

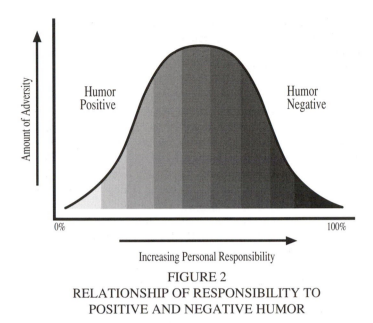

FIGURE 2
RELATIONSHIP OF RESPONSIBILITY TO
POSITIVE AND NEGATIVE HUMOR

It invited black audiences to accept images of themselves and remain content with their lot in life. Thus, such humor was negative.

The most heinous example I know regarding negative humor relates to the transportation of the Jews to their death in Nazi gas chambers. On a few occasions, the SS officers lured their unsuspecting Jewish passengers off the train and into the gas chambers by feigning comedy and using solicitous humor. They bowed low, played with their voices, and—almost like court jesters—gamboled around the loading ramp. Their humor reduced their own anxiety and raised a little hope in the minds of the Jews. It made the crowd easier to handle. The use of humor in this situation was negative in the extreme. Its evil effects promoted genocide and stunned the world community.

President Reagan was wounded in a assassination attempt. When going to the operating room, he offered many one-liners to diminish the anxiety of all concerned. To his surgery team he quipped: "I hope you're all Republican." In his adversity, he used humor to great advantage not only for himself but for the country as a whole. Part of his popularity as a President resulted from his timely use of humor. His use of humor in the operating room was positive.

I was told the following story by a female therapist who performs group therapy with adult women who have survived incest in their childhoods. These women bear terrible psychological scars from this adversity. Adversity which was visited upon them when they had no defense and no way out. They often have eating disorders, substance abuse problems, depression, sexual dysfunctions, and a deep distrust of intimacy. Many have no sense of humor. During childhood, fear and shame crowded out joy and laughter. They have a difficult time laughing at jokes or ever laughing at themselves. It's hard to take yourself lightly after a childhood filled with abuse.

In her group, the women were overcoming their problems and supporting one another well. One day, they decided they needed to lighten up if they were going to make it through. They wanted this group to become their laughing place as well as their crying place. They came up with a joke that was special for them. It became a one-liner to rely on when the going was rough. They knew humor would be good for them. This is their joke:

What's the difference between a prostitute, a mistress, and a housewife when the man she is having sex with just completes his sexual orgasm?

The prostitute proclaims: "That's all!!!"

The mistress queries: "That's all???"

The housewife muses: "Beige....I believe I'll paint the ceiling beige."

Whenever the feelings have been painful and one of them has grappled with one more step in her healing, another may hold her and say, "Beige..." It is loving, gentle, lighthearted, and it seems to help. It is their private joke. It is positive humor.

Do you have a laughing place? When the foxes and bears in your life beset you, do you have a place where you can go to laugh? Remember Brother Rabbit ("Brer" means "brother").

Your laughing place may be a real one or just one in your mind. Real or not, you need it. Create your laughing place now if you don't already have one. Make it real enough so you can retire there whenever needed—just by closing your eyes. And how about a joke of your own? One that will help you handle adversity and take yourself lightly at the same time? You need it, too.

CHAPTER VII

Fine Tuning

*Distinguishing Positive
From Negative Humor*

Humor heals and humor hurts. Humor loves and humor attacks. Humor plays and humor is cruel. Humor reflects the best and the worst of human beings. If you want to use humor in the service of healing, love, and play, you must understand how to distinguish positive from negative humor. The effects of humor often demonstrate whether it was positive or negative. Such effects depend on the intent of the sender and on the perception of the receiver. Be clear with your intentions. If somebody seems hurt or offended, your unconscious mind may be expressing hostile feelings you would like to deny. Assess your audience; be sensitive to their systems of forbiddens. Also continue to beware of jerks and fault finders. Sometimes your warmest intentions will be twisted by someone who is bent on being angry and offended.

The following nine criteria form the basis of assessing whether some particular humor is positive or negative. These don't determine whether humor "works" or not (that will be covered in the next chapter). These are criteria for judging whether humor has a positive or a negative result.

1.) Positive humor reduces anxiety for *every person* involved in the process. At least, nobody is the worse for it. Negative humor may have an unwilling victim (e.g. teasing or some ethnic joke) who feels increasing distress as a result of the process.

In a hospital emergency room, the staff often use quips and banter to buoy one another through heavy moments: "I need two units of whole blood and a Miller Lite, stat." That's fine, providing they are careful about who overhears them. A macabre quip could be positive among [just] the staff—but it becomes negative as soon as one person overhears it who doesn't understand and has his anxiety raised by their remarks. Always beware of fallout. Otherwise positive humor instantly may become negative when one person is jolted by perceived insensitivity.

2.) Positive humor brings people closer together both physically and psychologically. Recall some wonderful humor experience when you laughed well. You probably leaned toward a companion and maybe even touched. But when humor is negative, people turn away and look away. Physical distance and psychological distance both increase.

When somebody tells an offensive joke, you wish you could disappear or that the teller was moving to Siberia. You convey your feelings by turning away, rolling your eyes, and sighing.

3.) Positive humor enhances communication. As I watch people begin to laugh generously, they start talking with all the other people near them—even if they don't know one another. When humor is negative, silence happens; an uncomfortable, pregnant pause—a pause that fails to refresh.

During the humor workshop, I instruct the participants in gelastolalia. When they turn to one another and practice, it takes five minutes to get them to shut up. Once they start laughing, they start chattering as well. Positive humor always results in more and better communication.

74

4.) Positive humor helps people accept new ideas and information. For just that reason, humor—both positive and negative—is employed in selling, teaching, and debate.

Positive humor is a marvelously effective teaching device. The best classroom teachers may not be comedians, but they invariably have a warm accepting sense of humor. They encourage their students to laugh with the surprise of discovery and to play with their creativity. They help their students to avoid taking themselves too seriously, thus preventing anxiety from interfering in the learning process. The worst teachers use sarcasm, humiliation, and teasing. They may get a laugh, but often at a victim's expense.

Humor has been used by countless salesmen throughout history in order to open the mind—and the pocketbook—of a potential customer. My father was a travelling salesman. When I went "on the road" with him, he always kept a supply of new jokes on hand. I watched as customers listened to his stories and then remembered they had something they needed to order from him. He claimed it was the key to being successful. There is a narrow path to walk here; if a salesman uses humor to sell you overpriced swampland in Florida, that humor would be negative.

When defensiveness is a barrier to friendship or cooperation, positive humor provides an ideal solution. But, be careful, do not give up all your defenses too quickly, that could be naive. There are jerks in the world who would take advantage of your vulnerability; they might misinterpret your humorous intent and ridicule you. Positive humor does not mean being naive. Manage your humor wisely. And on the other hand, beware that some individual's intentions are not very noble, and their use of (negative) humor is intended to disarm you for their personal advantage. Positive humor does not suspend clear thinking while you enjoy a laugh.

5.) Positive humor surprises the listener with a new perspective, while negative humor depends on stereotypes and prejudice. Positive humor breaks down prejudice; it causes previously unacknowledged truths to become obvious.

I caught a taxi in Chicago. The driver started chattering.

Within a minute he told me he was Polish. "It's not easy to be humble when you're Polish—The Pope and the winner of the Noble Peace Prize in two years. Not bad, huh?" He was speaking of Lech Walesa and Pope John Paul II; both Polish, both honored by the world for their intelligence, integrity, and leadership. That line should break a few stereotypes.

6.) Positive humor depends on permission. Jokes require a target, whether it is an idea, an institution, or a person. If you are the target of some kidding or the butt of some joke, such joking can be positive *providing you accept that position willingly.* When victims are unwilling, they get hurt, and the humor is negative. However, if you will not accept any kidding at all, if no person can tease you about anything no matter how inconsequential, you are taking yourself too seriously.

Make a list of three things (at least) that you are willing to be kidded about. Then, make sure your loved ones and colleagues know what they are. When you understand this concept, change the list once a month or the teasing could get really stale.

My wife and children can tease with me about my evolving baldness, my funny feet with toes that don't touch the ground, and my perfectionism in dishwasher loading.

7.) Positive humor invites people in. The circle of laughter always enlarges to include those on the periphery. Negative humor excludes people. Private jokes put barriers between people. On occasion, some humor may need to remain private to avoid stepping over another's forbidden boundary. But when private jokes repetitively exclude others in a given setting, they are negative.

Cliques depend on privacy in order to exclude others thought, for whatever reason, to be inferior. One way of being exclusive is to keep a supply of private jokes. If you find yourself in such a situation, break the boundary, invite outsiders in. Laugh with them, make eye contact, physically turn your body to face them, and then remember you are doing your work in life in the process.

8.) Positive humor moves you in the direction of good health. Negative humor results in stress with all of its attendant miseries. Sticks and stones may break your bones, and names (negative humor) will make you ill, both physically and psychologically. Laughter alone doesn't heal. Positive humor coupled with laughter and blended with love and altruism, does.

9.) Positive humor is free. The best of humor, like the best of love, isn't for sale. The comedy you buy when you go to a nightclub is not negative *per se,* but the humor you spontaneously share with loved ones, friends, or co-workers is the positive ideal. Such humor is free and friendly. Comedians may entertain you, but they rarely enhance your quality of life. Laughter with friends and family is one key element in the quality of your life. During the waning hours of life, you will remember the moments of laughter with loved ones and you will smile.

An understanding of positive and negative humor should be incorporated into your belief system, into your perspective before you start experimenting with new behavior. To start with, apply this information in retrospect. Make a list of humorous events in your life—both positive and negative—and humorous people—both positive and negative. Then look at the nine criteria and notice how they permit you to distinguish positive from negative humor. You probably had some intuitive sense regarding the negative quality of some humor, now you have criteria for understanding the difference. Once you have surveyed your life experiences in retrospect, you are prepared to meet your future ones in new, creative, and more positive ways. This information will free you to make positive humor an art form. Master the techniques, and then forget them.

CHAPTER VIII

But Does It "Work"?

Necessary Ingredients
for Successful Humor

Sometime in your life you probably tried to be funny and the effort failed. People groaned or maybe they just looked at you in a curious, silent way. Maybe you risked appearing foolish, and your listeners, instead of appreciating your efforts, laughed *at* you. You felt humiliated and inside your head a little voice said, "Don't ever try that again. You really don't have a sense of humor." You agreed and decided forever to abandon efforts at humor for fear of embarrassment. That fear of appearing foolish and being ridiculed—either by laughter or by silence—is the most important overall inhibitor of your humor experience.

If your humor fails to generate a laugh, assess the four ingredients that are essential to making it work:

> Relationship
> Rapport
> Setting
> Timing

All four are important and must be considered; failure to account for any one can cause your attempt to fail.

Don't let this seem too complicated. At first, you may be wondering how you can play with any humor at all if you have to keep all four in mind all at once. It is like driving a car: Once you know the mechanics of vehicle operation and the rules of the road, it all becomes second nature. If you decide to commit yourself to practicing positive humor, you need to keep these four ingredients in mind. Later on, the process will become second nature. You won't have to consciously think about it.

All relationships have a potential for humor, once some rapport is established. But the setting will have to be conducive also. Then when humor is timed properly, it works and rapport is enhanced and the relationship flourishes.

When I was first assigned as a flight surgeon to the Marines, I had social responsibilities that went with my job. As the base flight surgeon, I reported to the Commanding General and I had to include him on invitation lists for social gatherings. We came to know each other in a stiff, formal sort of way. I respected him greatly; he dealt fairly with his men. My wife and I decided to take a big risk and invite the General and his wife to dinner, just the two of them. We decided to get to know them as people. There was a vast gulf of rank separating us—in the Marine Corps rank makes a lot of difference. I was a Navy Lieutenant and he was a One Star General.

We made the house spic and span, and my wife planned the best meal possible. We awoke our boys (aged nine months and two and a half years) early in the morning and made it a full day for them. Short naps and then a full afternoon at the swimming pool. An hour before the General arrived, we fed them a high carbohydrate meal and then gave them a long, leisurely warm bath. Our younger son went out like a light. Our older son was wired, he knew something was up. We put him down five minutes before the General arrived.

There was a knock at the door.

"Good evening, General,...Ma'am"

As they stepped in our front door, my son came out in his diaper. He looked up at the strangers and smiled. He walked up to the General and took one thick finger in his small hand and uttered his newest words, "Vacuum cleaner."

The graying, handsome, Korean War fighter ace, Brigadier General of the United States Marine Corps followed as my son walked him to the one "off-limits" room of the whole apartment—Fibber McGee's closet, the large hall closet where everything goes at the last minute to make the place look like House Beautiful. They opened the door and a few things fell out. Within minutes we three adults were sitting in the living room as my son and the General moved the furniture around and vacuumed the carpet once again. The General was laughing so hard, tears were in his eyes. Our reservations gave way to relief.

His wife smiled and she cried silent tears too. Her smile mixed in a deep sadness. "This is the first time I have seen him laugh in two months. Ever since our oldest son was shot down over Hanoi. He is MIA."

Later on my son went to bed. We talked into the wee hours. We laughed, we joked, we had some very serious moments, we became friends. The next day, I met him as he came around for inspection. I saluted and greeted him, "Good Morning, General." We didn't engage in a humorous exchange then. The setting called for something else. Our formality didn't nullify the love and laughter of the previous evening. It didn't mean that we wouldn't joke again. It was a setting where something else was required.

All relationships may involve humor. When the relationship involves a subordinate role for one participant, the person in authority needs to initiate the humor. If the boss laughs, everyone laughs. If the boss is neurotic, the organization will be neurotic. A little rapport is essential at first, and thereafter rapport is enhanced by the appropriate use of humor.

Between equals, i.e. friends, family members, or lovers, humor may be initiated by anyone. Generally, in such relationships, a pattern evolves in which one person is more the performer and the other, the audience. This can shift often. Both roles are important to humor in a relationship, but perhaps the one who takes the role of audience is more important. The one who laughs or appreciates the other's attempts at humor is giving a gift that is very loving. *The gift of laughter is a loving gift.*

Pay particular attention to the setting when you practice

positive humor. Humor intended as positive may at the same time be perceived as negative if the attempt is overheard by an observer whose anxiety level is increased by the joke. Law enforcement personnel are prone to this mistake. They often use a macabre sort of humor that sustains them through terrible tragedies. It's OK when the humor is among themselves only. It becomes negative if a bystander overhears the comment and feels worse on account of it. The policeman who is investigating a fatal auto accident picks up a nearly disembodied arm and remarks when looking at the still functional wrist watch, "Takes a licking and keeps on ticking." His comment may sustain him and his buddy but could be material for a lawsuit by a grieving companion of the dead person.

This principle also applies in one of the last bastions of gross humor, the operating room. Evidence is accumulating that anesthetized patients can actually hear what is going on. It doesn't mean that no humor should be exchanged; it just means that the patient shouldn't be the butt of the joke. For the same reason, the punch line shouldn't imply a dreadful outcome. Patients have been known to go into cardiac arrest upon "hearing" some comment that could be interpreted as predicting a disastrous outcome. Personally I would like my surgeon to know some good M*A*S*H punch lines—meaningful, funny, and politically liberal.

Finally, timing is probably the most difficult part of humor to apply. Herein lies the art of the process. First, allow enough time for the imagination to work. Never rush a punch line. Of course, the other extreme can be excruciating—the guy who drags the joke out for so long, you have long since guessed the punch line or you really don't care any more. Second, remember the non-verbal, interactive pathway to humor. Be aware of your face as you tell your stories and pause for effect. Make eye contact and use your facial expression as a vehicle of suspense. Watch a good comedian, notice how he uses his face to enhance the timing of his routine. Timing without attention to facial expression is mechanical and unlikely to work.

Take time now and apply this information to your own life. Make a list of your relationships that include humor and those that do not. Do you want to include more humor in one of them? If the answer is yes, ask yourself first about the quality of rapport in the relationship. If the rapport is good, enhancing humor is quite simple if you choose the setting with care. If the rapport is not good, increase your eye contact and use your face for non-verbal interactions. Smile more frequently and relax your shoulders and forehead. Make sure you are aware of the forbiddens of the other person; take care not to violate them. Again ask yourself about what setting would be best for humor to work. Act as if the targeted individual already has a sense of humor, and you are just helping him rediscover it. After all, that is the truth of the matter.

CHAPTER IX

Hi–Ho Zygomaticus

*The Seven Steps of Humor
Expression*

The zygomaticus major is not a Greek military officer, it is the primary smiling muscle. Connected from your cheekbone (the zygoma) to the corners of your mouth, it pulls up the corners of your mouth as the first muscular expression of a humor response. Then a sequence follows that expresses your humor experience from the mildest amusement to laughing-till-you-cry. There are seven steps in the process. Of course, they overlap and in some situations, you may leave out a step now and then. My intention is to teach you the steps of humor expression so you can incorporate this knowledge into your daily humor practice. The principle relates to the concept of biofeedback. What your facial musculature does—or your whole body for that matter—affects how you feel. By expressing a feeling, you change it; if it is positive, usually you enhance it. By suppressing the expression of a feeling, you suppress the experience of it. In time you may extinguish the awareness of a feeling altogether by suppressing its expression. Of course, that doesn't mean it's gone for good. It continues to lurk in your unconscious seeking another way out.

Expressing humor is what gelastolalia is all about. I introduced you to gelastolalia in Chapter V. If something strikes you as funny, express the feeling. In fact, the more willing you are to express your humor, the more you will experience it. It is simple behavioral psychology.

You might wonder why I coined the word, "gelastola- lia". The idea came to me as a result of having studied sex therapy in the early seventies. I took a course on the treatment of sexual dysfunctions in Los Angeles. (Not a bad place to study sexual dysfunctions.) A concept that we were taught was "erolalia." Es- sentially it means that if you are feeling good in the process of a sexual experience, make appropriate sounds to express your pleasure and you will enhance your own experience and that of your partner as well. Perhaps you first experienced sexual pleasure in circumstances that were not conducive to making much noise. Or, if you have raised small children you know how—for years at a time—you suppress all the sounds of love making. Right in the middle of your highest pleasure, you keep one ear open for possible observers and then if you are getting carried away, you try to quiet down. You begin to go over your shopping list or think of putting the garbage out. Little wonder the experience loses its zip after a while.

There is a story about a couple in Southern California who were having sexual problems in their marriage. In essence, he was not doing his share. Just taking care of himself and "selling her short"—as it were. Anyway, she took him to a sex therapist and they had some therapy. Southern California is an interesting part of the country for many reasons. Among other things, they have earthquakes there. The tremors jolt or roll and they can last from a couple seconds to over a minute. Their intensity is measured on the Richter Scale. Over 5 implies property damage; over 6, the loss of life. Well, this couple went home to their house in the San Fernando Valley. They went to work on their erolalia assignment just as an earthquake measur- ing 6.2 on the Richter Scale hit. It was a "roller" and it lasted for a minute and a half. Their bed began to roll back and forth across the room, smashing the furniture. Finally it crashed out through the wall and fell onto the front lawn. The woman looked up at her mate and said with satisfied smile, "Now that's what I had in mind."

Sex has good press and high expectations. Humor does

too. With gelastolalia, I can't guarantee you an earthquake, but I can guarantee it is one of the concepts that can help you change your humor experience. It will provide you with specific behaviors to incorporate into your life, behaviors you can start employing today. With luck, the responses of others to your new behaviors will encourage you to continue the process. Here is how the seven steps of the zygomaticus progression work out. Master these and you will become an advanced practitioner of gelastolalia—a gelastolologist.

Step 1. The smile. When you contract only the zygomaticus major, you manifest what is called an insincere smile. No other muscles in your face work. Gravity just pulls your face down as it always does, while only the corners of your mouth draw up. It's the kind of smile you get when an unfriendly co-worker greets you back after an absence, "Glad you're back." Or from a cool boss, "I know you're doing the best you can." Try it in front of a mirror. Look at yourself and only turn up the corners of your mouth. Doesn't do much for you does it? Yet for the truly dreary people of this world, this is the full extent of humor expression they allow themselves.

Step 2. The twinkle. Other muscles of your face get involved in the zygomaticus progression, especially the sheath of muscles encircling the eyes—the orbicularis oculi. (The use of such words should ally any doubts you may have had about my being a *bona fide* physician, M.D. type.) The orbicularis squinches your eyes up causing the smile to appear sincere. Think of the orbicularis oculi as the "Clint Eastwood muscle"—after all, it is the only muscle on his face that works. It is also the muscle that causes crows feet. Again, look at yourself in the mirror and smile first and then add a twinkle. If you won't get up and go to a mirror, do it right now and see how it feels. Better than Step 1, huh?

Step 3. The clown face. This is a hard one to try without somebody demonstrating it. The frontalis (forehead muscle) pulls the face up, while the platysma (lower face and superficial neck muscle) pulls it down. This is a smile you make when you don't care how crazy you look. It is full on silly. Usually the jaw opens a bit and the teeth and tongue are exposed. Try this if you dare, but don't do so if you're riding the subway while reading this. You may be misinterpreted. No telling what somebody might presume while you are making such a face.

Step 4. The giggle. When you first start to laugh, you let out only small amounts of air and therefore sound. Just the upper chest muscles work. The full smile is usually operating. If it isn't, the process is called a chuckle. There is quite a gender difference in this form of expression. Giggling isn't macho. Real men might eat quiche on occasion, but they *never* giggle. After all, giggling is what teenage girls do to alleviate anxiety. Almost enough to make listeners swear off giggling forever. Try a giggle now with a full clown smile. If you feel ridiculous, rest assured that everybody does when they do this with no humor stimulus.

Step 5. The (belly) laugh. Now is when it gets good. But before you get into belly laughing, consider some of the design considerations that God had to make in the process of creating this creature that would laugh. With full belly laughter, air is expressed through a partially closed glottis (wind pipe apparatus) at a speed of up to seventy miles per hour. In order to prevent serious consequences, the first muscle to be engaged in the process is the anal sphincter—it tightens. The reasons should be obvious. In fact the whole sling of muscles down there at the other end of the pelvis tightens—it has to or laughing would be severely limited for public health reasons.

The head is best thrown back slightly, any constricting garments around the neck loosened, and the hands placed on the belly (your own belly preferably) Santa Claus style. Then it's either ho-ho or ha-ha, rarely he-he which is more of a giggling sound. There is a gender difference on this one too. Men are more free to use this expression. Women usually cover their mouths and lean forward to stifle this form of laughter, except those women who are overweight *and accept themselves that way.* It's not an all-or-none thing, but it is a correlation that I have observed. I think that in the middle ages, women who laughed freely were thought to be prostitutes, and those who didn't laugh freely were seen as saintly. Too bad. Perhaps if we had let women laugh freely with their bellies, there would be fewer of them with eating disorders. I have never met the anorexic who laughed freely.

Step 6. Move and strike. If something is hilarious and you are free to express yourself, you will begin to move back and forth; you may slap yourself, stomp the floor, or even hit the people near you—or lean on them at least. Positive humor diminishes the distance between people. At this stage, endorphins are flowing freely and you are in the midst of one of life's most pleasurable moments. It's good for you. Most people are limited by the fear that they will appear retarded or unsophisticated if they express themselves this way. The setting makes a difference, but many people would never consider this form of humor expression in *any* setting. Where will you allow yourself such complete expression? When did you last laugh so well? With whom would you like to laugh this well in the near future? Maybe you should try it. What do you think?

Step 7. Crying. The final step involves a behavior that is often associated with sadness. With laughter this intense, tears flow freely and you become exhausted. Not uncommonly, you will begin to feel a variety of emotions besides humor. Probably the neurotransmitters in your brain are "overflowing" (so to say) and causing you to experience several emotions at one time. At this point the humor experience runs out. Limp and weary, you plead for whoever is causing you to laugh, to please stop, they're killing you! This is intense enough that most people don't want to experience it too often.

Incidentally, there is a converse side to the laugh/cry relationship that is worth mentioning. Some persons, on receiving tragic news such as the death of a loved one, may laugh instead of cry. Again it is probably due to neurotransmitter misdirection. It does not necessarily mean hysteria or denial. Such people need to be encouraged to express their laughter and, when so encouraged, the tears will follow in moments. It is part of a grief process.

Medical research is revealing some unusual information about the physiology of crying as the final expression of laughter. There is an immune substance present in all tears which is called d-lysozyme. In the tears of laughter it is more concentrated. We wonder if it represents enhanced immunity as a result of free laughter. The idea is intriguing, but requires more study. It brings to mind the verse from Proverbs (17:22), "A merry heart doeth like a good medicine, but a brittle spirit drieth the bones." I can't guarantee improved immunity, but history and recent scientific propositions certainly recommend humor as a medicine. We know depression suppresses many immune processes and may leave the body more vulnerable to cancer or infection. It only stands to reason that positive laughter will enhance immunity.

How can this knowledge help you? You need to learn the seven steps and go over them until you can distinguish each of them. Then when you have your next spontaneous humor experience, *add one more step*. Every time you find something funny, give yourself permission to take a chance and express yourself more completely. By expressing this positive feeling, you will enhance it. You will begin to feel that you have a better sense of humor. People who share your life will think so too. Practice for six weeks and the change will be solid. The "new you" *will* have a better sense of humor. After all, we have agreed that humor is made up of perception and behavior. You will have succeeded in changing both.

CHAPTER X

Grow Up, Get Serious

*How humor is extinguished in growth
and development*

There is a "razor's edge" issue in this concept of how you diminish your sense of humor as you grow up. Too little humor leads to a dry, depressed existence. Too much humor interferes with getting necessary work done. And when humor is negative, it often hurts others. Being serious is a biological reality of adult life. This is most appropriate since the work wouldn't get done if we had to rely on the attention spans of kids with their tendency to "horse around." The most difficult workshop I ever presented was to a junior high school, seven hundred early adolescents—a sea of bodies that never stopped moving. They liked to laugh, but it took five minutes to get their attention again. At no time did I have one hundred percent of their attention. I am in awe of those souls who have elected to teach junior high kids. Either they are serving out some punishment for something terrible in a past life or they are racking up lots of credits for the future.

Psychotherapists encounter burned out adults all the time. Blue and tired out, these "grown ups" experience almost no joy in the process of being alive. Humor and laughter are dim memories associated with "the good old days." These adults don't reminisce about wealth or ease, rather they recall friendship and shared laughter. Too often, the process of growing up and getting serious leads to tedious daily living—not an appealing promise.

I don't suggest that we retain *all* the self-centered ready laughter of childhood. But, unfortunately, many successful adults have overcompensated in their pursuit of maturity and have relinquished more of their humor than necessary. How does this happen? How, at predictable stages during growth and development, was your good humor suppressed? Often parents and teachers in your life corrected you for laughing—be it in the wrong setting or at the wrong time. It was appropriate for them to do so. Other times it was not. And there were occasions when nobody inhibited you—you diminished your sense of humor all by yourself, without any conscious decision.

BABIES ARE DIFFERENT

This statement shouldn't seem too dramatic, but it flies in the face of a widely held contemporary belief that whatever is wrong in life is a result of the environment—usually the parents. Visit a newborn nursery and see how infants react to being hungry. Some are quiet, some mew little silent cries, some chew their fists, while others scream in rage. The difference is either genetic or a result of the intrauterine existence. I believe a lot more human behavior is influenced by genetics than we think. Humans take a long time to mature, and we are unable to control their environments in order to really test out the contribution of genetics.

Becoming a parent is like entering a crap shoot. There is a lot of luck in what you get. I have seen children from horrendous backgrounds succeed very well, and I have seen children with wonderful loving parents become criminal. I don't believe environment determines "the whole nine yards." Some children, for example, are born with a natural, positive sense of humor, while others have trouble laughing at all. Fortunately, the vast majority fall somewhere in between. I believe that what we call "a sense of humor" is distributed as a trait in the population following a natural distribution pattern, much like mathematic ability or the capacity to spell. Such skills do not necessarily depend on intelligence. Some very bright kids can't spell or handle algebra. But most kids can be taught to balance a checkbook and spell well enough to correspond meaningfully. Hence, everyone has the capacity to learn and develop an adequate sense of humor.

THE LAUGHING BABY

We have already discussed how the smiling response represents your first humor experience. How parents reinforce a baby for smiling and laughing will shape a vast amount of humor expression for the rest of life. The child that is ignored when it laughs and is only responded to when it cries will soon know how to get attention in life. Caretakers of infants should be consistent and should recognize that shared smiling and laughter are critical to healthy infant development.

THE UNHOLY ALLIANCE

Late in the first year of life aggression becomes more manifest. Human beings need to be aggressive; it is essential for our survival. Aggression has a large measure of selfishness in it. Children have such selfishness in abundance; we call it narcissism.

A fourteen month old toddler was able to coordinate walking and carrying something at the same time. His first mission was to carry his toy truck over and drop it on a sleeping cat. The cat jumped in surprise and the child laughed. He was amused as he was surprised. He was amused by his newfound mastery. And he was surprised by the results of his aggression. Older toddlers hit their playmates with little remorse, in fact they sometimes laugh with delight at the plaintive cries of their companions. Visit a preschool and observe the children. They often will act aggressively, and then they will laugh. In grade school physical aggression gradually gives away to verbal aggression as teasing develops. For many, verbal aggression and its accompanying derisive laughter persist well into adult life.

This unholy alliance between aggression and humor is a major inhibitor of positive humor throughout all of life. Aggression doesn't magically disappear; it persists. Humor continues to be experienced in conjunction with aggression. Thus aggression provides one of the primary underlying causes for negative humor. The self-centered child is amused by his capacity to inflict pain or discomfort on others. Grade school boys band together and scapegoat another unfortunate child. They laugh with derision at whatever defect they choose to be the target of their so-called humor. For example, a boy in the sixth grade starts having some prepubertal acne and is called "Toad" from that point on—even if his face clears up. Parents need to curb or redirect this aggression. The obedient child who responds to his parent's correction may think he is doing the right thing not only to curb his aggression but also to curb his humor. As he grows older he often is reminded: "Wipe that smile off your face!"

Rather than using anger or teasing to correct the child, you might use humor to divert the child's attention. When a five year old expresses glee at the pain he has inflicted on another child, avoid the tendency to inflict pain or ridicule as your punishment. Instead, encourage the child to see the situation from the perspective of the victim of his aggression. To use violence or the threat of violence to correct violent behavior fosters continued violence in the long run. Ridicule fosters the use of aggressive teasing late in life. In the case of physical violence, the child learns that violence becomes the prerogative of the strongest— not unlike our superpower mentality. In the case of ridicule, the child learns to become a critic, never satisfied with leaving well enough alone.

THE TERRIBLE TWO'S

Toilet training and the emergence of the forbiddens not only mark the second pathway for humor expression, they also provide for significant confusion. The child who plays with his genitals in a natural way may be scolded and told that he is immoral or sinful. The child who feels bad about himself when he has been punished will curtail such normal activity. As a parent, you have a legitimate objective in teaching morality and cleanliness and showing your child appropriate limits for the forbiddens. When possible, try to teach the importance of setting when explaining the forbiddens rather than just saying "no." Avoid attaching guilt or fear to the forbiddens. Remember that with each "no" laid down in the developing mind of a child, an opportunity for thinking about that "no" will stimulate a smile and trigger the second pathway to humor expression in that child's mind throughout childhood and on into adult life. With an older, verbal child, explain that topics of joking will vary from the campfire to the church basement; one setting almost encourages bawdy stories and the other proscribes it. Just as teaching empathy is the best method for helping a child to curb his aggression, so too, teaching sensitivity to other's feelings and the appropriateness of the setting is necessary for a child to understand when to joke about forbidden subjects.

NYEAH, NYEAH, NYEAH, NYEAH, NYEAH—CHILDHOOD TEASING

This is an extension of the unholy alliance but it involves a particular experience that occurs to teasing victims during grade school years. A child is teased by other children who are chanting anything that can get under his skin. When he finally breaks down and cries, one of the teasers comes up and says, "What's the matter, can't you take a joke?" Such a statement is a club. And we don't abandon these clubs after childhood. We use these tactics well into adult life to attack other people. During a tennis match when an overweight partner is struggling to keep up, his buddy quips, "You know, Fred, you don't sweat very much for a fat guy." In the mind of the victim he wonders, "I didn't find that funny. It hurt. I guess I don't have a sense of humor." In that case, laughter elicits a memory of personal pain. Little wonder we grow up to be sober and serious. Psychotic adults often hallucinate laughter and almost never is such laughter friendly and warm; it is usually ridiculing and derisive.

The goal for parents during this period is to teach children how to distinguish humor from aggression. They need to direct children toward humor in which no person is the victim. And the same goes for adults who are aggressive. I am often asked how to deal with adults who are hurtful and negative with their humor. Do I use humor to cut them down? Give them a dose of their own medicine? Certainly not. I confront them seriously and directly, stating that their humor is aggressive and negative. I will not demean my positive humor by taking it down to their level. Humor is too precious to be used to get even.

EMBARRASSMENT, PEER PRESSURE, AND JUNIOR HIGH

How many of you remember junior high as the best years of your life? Less than one percent. How many of you remember junior high as being the most painful years of your life? About forty percent. Junior high is a nightmare. In fact, *adolescence should be a diagnosable mental disorder*. It is a time of raging hormones, awkward physical growth, aligning with peers, and avoiding the family. Embarrassment is probably the most potent modifier of behavior at this age. Most junior high kids are embarrassed to have parents, "No, I don't have parents. I live in a box on the edge of town. My parents are in Australia."

Those kids who try to be funny and fail, deeply regret their attempt and decide never to try it again; they believe they have no sense of humor at all. Those who succeed at humor may be the class clowns, but they are often quite aggressive as well. It is a time that kids experiment with the macabre; they seek to use forbidden subjects in such a way as to draw the revulsion of any adult listener. They gleefully engage in "black market humor" to further separate themselves from the adult world. Recent examples include dead baby jokes, Ethiopian jokes, and AIDS stories. Unfortunately, there are some who never grow beyond this stage and continue their callous ways into adult life. Fortunately, they are easy to deal with; we call them "jerks."

TERMINAL COOL

With the advent of high school years, kids are trying to modify their childish ways and seek to do so by elevating passive-aggressiveness into an art form. They attempt to appear sophisticated and uninvolved. They not only want to avoid being part of the adult world, they are horrified to be confused with junior high "children." They may begin to appreciate adult humor, but they wouldn't want to be caught dead enjoying themselves with adults. The distance between parents and teenage children is a consequence of development. What parents wish could be a time for positive attachment is not. Rather, at this time, kids—independent of their parents—find a way to re-experience their infantile humorous ways and still be grown up. They find a way to play that is cool in a very special way. They aren't even afraid of being embarrassed. They discover alcohol.

HAPPY HOUR ISN'T

There is an ancient relationship between alcohol and humor. Throughout history it has been used not just to relax or forget troubles, *alcohol has been used as a primary means to access humor.* What do people say on Friday night? "I'm going to go out and poison myself a bit, risk my life driving a car, and spend an hour watching the water swish symmetrically around the white porcelain of a toilet bowl." No, they say, "I'm going to go out and *party.* I'm going out to have a few laughs."

Between sixteen and twenty, the relationship between alcohol and humor becomes apparent. Alcohol equals party which equals laughter which supposedly equals good humor. Later in life, if you go to Las Vegas to see a comedian perform, they won't let you buy just one drink. They know the more the audience drinks, the easier it is to make them laugh—and the more money they will spend. (As an aside, I believe it was W. C.

Fields who said: "A woman drove me to drink and I never had the courtesy to thank her.") There are people who never laugh unless they drink. Hence, one of the primary attractions to alcohol abuse is the desire to experience laughter. If you fail to appreciate humor while sober, you may turn to alcohol to "loosen up" and to laugh.

Alcoholism is a disease. About ten percent of our society suffers from it. Part of its treatment requires that you not drink alcohol any more. But that does not mean that you don't laugh any more. Treatment of alcoholism must include ways to help people reexperience humor while sober. Sobriety does not need to be dull. It can—and should—be fun, lighthearted, and even crazy. It just means you no longer use alcohol to deal with the world; not with your problems, not with your family, not with your laughter or lack of it.

Notice how many comedians in the past have included a drunk character in their comedy routines. Being a drunk was seen as funny. Fortunately, it is now being seen for the disease it is. During the later stages of the disease process, humor disappears completely—whether drunk or sober. A mark of recovery occurs when people regain their spontaneous ability to laugh. If you drink alcohol, ask yourself whether you laugh easily when you haven't been drinking. If you almost never laugh unless you have been drinking, you may be alcoholic. If so, talk to a close friend about it. Or talk to your physician or call AA—its number is in your nearest phone book.

SERIOUS BUSINESS

If you want to be taken seriously in your chosen career, you will probably want to be hard working and serious. That's fine. Positive humor is compatible with such goals. But most careers have strong limits on humor because the negative use of humor is so counterproductive. Most professions view humor with suspicion since negative humor use has concealed ignorance or laziness. Humor, negatively applied, has been used to waste time and has diverted workers from legitimate problem solving activity. Joke swapping or horseplay is psychologically rewarding and often more enjoyable than work, especially when the task is tedious and boring. Any supervisor knows that a "tight ship" is necessary, or control of the setting will be lost and productivity will drop.

The positive humor proposition regarding laughter in the workplace sees humor as a spice—a little goes a long way. It livens up the place, smoothes communication, and even promotes creativity. Later in the book, you will find specific applications for positive humor use in the workplace.

Unfortunately, the enlightened appreciation of positive humor is lacking in most settings including my profession of psychiatry. During my educational process, I had to be very careful. Freud made it perfectly clear that if you are joking, you have some unfulfilled sexual desire or some unexpressed aggression. (O.K., who doesn't?) Inappropriate play and negative humor ought to be prohibited, but spicing up the work place with positive humor is likely to enhance productivity and reduce employee sick time. The key is in distinguishing positive from negative humor.

MATING, DATING, AND MARRIAGE

The order of these three ideas reflects that we are in the eighties. There is an interesting relationship between humor and how you go about attracting a mate. There is even a more interesting relationship between humor and having a healthy marriage.

I once reviewed the files of a video dating service. Clients were asked to list the qualities they most valued in a person they would like to date. Statistically, the most common trait being sought after was a sense of humor. It occurred more frequently in the first three characteristics listed than did any other; more frequently than good looks, money, leisure time activities, or religious orientation. Humor is one of the principle ways we attract others to us. It is a trait we look for in a mate. Hence we put on a certain "humor face" while in the dating market. It doesn't necessarily represent who we really are, but it is necessary for being selected. Later on, when we get to know the other well enough, we let down our front and introduce them to "the real me."

During marriage, humor often diminishes because of numerous reasons—but often primarily because the process of attraction is over. I have counselled at least a thousand couples in which one member has had an affair. It is interesting that, though sex is a big part of it, they speak more fondly of laughing with the other person, of being able to be like a child with him/her. They feel safe, they laugh a lot.

The characteristics that make a marriage successful can be summed up as: 1.) My spouse is my best friend. (Ever had a best friend you didn't laugh with?) 2.) I respect my spouse as a person. That is, I respect how my spouse is doing his/her work in life. 3.) Marriage is a sacred commitment or at least a life long promise. 4.) We agree on what is important in life. 5.) We laugh together. This information, modified from an article in *Psychology Today* (June, 1985) "Marriages Made to Last" by Lauer and Lauer, ranked sexual adjustment much lower than shared laughter in providing cohesion in a marriage. That being the case, you will readily agree that we need to counsel couples to laugh together—certainly as much as we counsel them to make love well. Many sex therapists earn very good money fixing up sex lives. Perhaps we need some humor therapists too?

TRY BECOMING A PARENT

If you haven't lost your sense of humor by early adult life, try becoming a parent. Talk about getting serious. You have to be guide, guru, protector, provider, and teacher about such things as gastrointestinal tracts and the divine mysteries behind the universe. It is very easy to become negative in the process of parenting. You often find yourself saying "no" to almost anything. Kids seem to sense that you feel bad about yourself when saying "no." So they decide to help with your spiritual development and they ask for more things that can only be answered with a "no." And you are afraid that if you laugh at any of their attempts at forbidden humor, you will cause them to grow up to be immoral.

I came home one day to find my sons and six other teenage boys laughing and looking very embarrassed. Their silence and suppressed giggles suggested I investigate what was happening. Finally they produced a recent addition of one of those joke books filled with tasteless and dirty jokes. They were in stitches and they were afraid I would reprimand them. I looked at the book; the jokes were offensive to women, all ethnic groups and religions, and degraded sex to something below an overripe septic tank. What is a father to do? Well, I remembered my own advice, "Establish rapport first, then preach second." I sat down, asked them to show me the "best" jokes, and then I read them out loud slowly and with great eye contact. They were clever and they were negative. After the laughter died down and the rapport was established, I made my pitch about positive humor. I asked them to imagine growing up female, black, or hispanic and then honestly tell me how they would feel. We had a good talk. I have not seen the book since.

The trick with humor in the parenting process is trying to say "yes" fifty percent of the time. Seventy percent is better. Make every effort to laugh with your children as they are growing up. To laugh well early in life may diminish the need for "tough love" in adolescence. Hopefully, humor can supplant money as a major bond between parents and maturing children. (Bumper sticker quote: "Money isn't everything, but it sure helps the children stay in touch.")

TOO, TOO BUSY

The middle years of life are supposed to be your most productive. Your career is peaking and your income is reaching its maximum. And it is a time when you are responsible for aging parents and minor children. Children are becoming teenagers and test your remaining humor every day. Regardless of how much you earn, money is always a problem and leisure time a luxury. Humor becomes the most expendable part of life. It is crowded out in preference for getting the work done. Often alcohol is sought for relaxation. Little wonder these are the years when depression becomes so frequent.

Frazzled forty year olds sometimes come to my office thinking they need a rest and wonder if they need treatment in a psychiatric hospital. "Doctor, every hour is so full. There is always someone who needs something from me. When I finally have some time, I can't get my mind to shut off. It just keeps running, running, running. I wake up earlier than I need to and hit the floor at a full run." I assess their problems and if I fail to diagnose a psychiatric disorder, I frequently prescribe time off at the beach rather than in a hospital. No wrist watches, no schedules, no calendar. They need time. They suffer from hurry up sickness. The time they need is for relaxation and for play, and perhaps some therapeutic introspection. I assign exercises to help them incorporate humor into everyday life.

If you don't cultivate your humor experience during your middle years, don't expect to acquire it with a gold watch at retirement. Many people are disappointed at retirement because they forgot how to laugh. They even forgot why they used to laugh. Retirement often becomes a lethal condition for such individuals.

TOO LONELY

In our culture, there is a tendency to segregate elder folks and have little to do with them. Many are too lonely to have fun. Many lost their humor as they traversed the stages of development from being a laughing baby to serious adulthood. (You could consider the process one of becoming "adulterated.") Even with senility encroaching, humor is still possible. Older people can laugh by reminiscing about memories of humorous moments. Life for the elderly is often retrospective. The forbiddens still can stimulate a laugh. And the last pathway to be lost in senility is the non-verbal interactive one. You only have to make eye contact with an oldster and then let your faces play.

Of course, you must have some rapport and the setting has to be right. (Let's not forget relationship, rapport, setting, and timing.)

A friend sent me this short piece which does a nice job of weaving some humor into the aging experience. Most old folks I know have enjoyed it.

I am an elderly lady and I live alone; but I don't get lonely because I have some men friends who keep me company. I wake up with Charley Horse. I eat with Will Power. I spend the day with Arthur Ritis. And I go to bed with Ben Gay.

Things are not the same anymore. Everything is so much farther away than it used to be. It is twice as far to the corner, and they have added a hill. I have given up running for the bus—it moves faster than it used to. And they are making stairs steeper than in the good old days. Have you noticed the smaller print they now use in the newspaper? There is no sense in asking anyone to read aloud—everyone speaks in such a low voice that I can hardly hear a word.

Even people are changing...They are so much younger than they used to be when I was their age. On the other hand, people of my age are so much older than I. I ran into a classmate the other day and she had aged so much she didn't recognize me. I got to thinking about the poor thing while I was combing my hair this morning, and in doing so, I glanced at my reflection—and confound it, they don't make mirrors the way they used to!

SO NOW WHAT?

You have just reviewed a brief survey of human growth and development. Whole courses are taught in college and books are written on any one of these stages. The intention here is for you to have a framework for understanding your own humor experience in light of your own history. If you want to, you can survey your life now and come to terms with how your sense of humor was shaped.

1.) Make some guess about your humor genes. Are you intrinsically a humorous person?

2.) What do you know about your earliest two years of life? Who was there to smile with you and play with you?

3.) How strict was your family about issues of toilet training and messiness in general?

4,) Make a chart of your life, dividing it into natural stages. For example, grade school could be a stage, or the time after you moved, or when a parent was ill. Then recall what humor experiences you had in each stage, good and bad. Ask yourself what they did to your concept of humor and your concept of yourself.

5.) Look at each stage and notice who was a positive humor figure and who was a negative one. Whom do you most resemble today?

6.) Is there anything you would like to change? You can't change the past, but you can use your understanding of the past to undertake change today. If you wish to change something, make sure it is behavioral—so you can measure whether you are changing it or not.

In this way you can make use of this information to help you change your perspective and your behavior. Ideally you will be able to find two or three behaviors or perspectives you will want to change and are within reasonable reach. Later in the book, you will learn specific techniques that you may use in your personal humor process.

CHAPTER XI

Wellness Pie

Humor for the Best of Health

Working in the Emergency Room, I often came across a situation that frustrated me. Presented with a patient who had a medical complaint, I would ask whether he had been in good health. He would respond with "Dr. Harlow *gave* me a physical. So sure, I guess I'm pretty healthy."

First of all, I'm sure his doctor didn't *give* him anything, she charged him for it. A physical isn't a gift, it's an observation. I tried to explain to my patients that they could walk out and drop dead five minutes after a physical—a physical examination is not a guarantee of good health. Since then, the holistic movement has helped provide ways of enhancing future good health. It has encouraged individuals to make positive choices to live healthier lives and placed the responsibility where it belongs—with the individual, not his doctor.

The concept of "wellness" suggests that there is a spectrum of good health that exists beyond merely being not-sick. It implies that you can achieve vigorous good health, that you can live abundantly. Proponents of wellness suggest approaches that break life into component parts and then offer specific techniques to improve each. Ultimately, a whole is created which is greater than the sum of its component parts.

Almost all such formulae include a good sense of humor some-where in the process. Rarely, however, are there instructions of how and where to implement humor.

Now that you understand the broad definition of humor and can distinguish between positive and negative humor, you can apply these concepts to a wellness lifestyle. Figure 1 is a pie graph that represents six components of wellness. Rather than being a separate piece of the wellness pie, humor is a component of each constituent part.

THE WELLNESS PIE
FIGURE 1

AEROBIC EXERCISE

Exercise can be of great benefit to your health, but if you become too serious and self-critical, you can end up the worse for the effort. Humor—positive, easy-going humor—is the ingredient missing when people let exercise get the best of them.

Jogging, biking, swimming, walking, aerobics are all good for you. Any particular one may not be good for you specifically, but in general they give your heart a work-out, reduce stress, keep you strong, improve your circulation, lower your body weight, and probably diminish your likelihood of dying from a heart attack. All that sounds pretty good. But how about the people who exercise too much? Consider the "obligatory athletes"—those people who are negatively addicted to exercise. For example, such individuals who are runners may run to the exclusion of personal relationships. They run in spite of injury. They are preoccupied with lean body mass. They only want to talk about running and races. They value only those people who have similar interests. They run even when it is not good for them. They have serious problems with intimacy and difficulty expressing anger. And they have little or no sense of humor. They have all the psychological characteristics of people who suffer from anorexia nervosa. If such individuals had taken their humor running with them, they may have prevented their compulsive problems.

Being easy going and non-self critical may not be appropriate for olympic athletes or professionals, especially while engaged in competition. They need that critical edge and narrowly focused attention. But those who fail to find their humor elsewhere often end up, like so many famous athletes, with serious drug problems. Perhaps many of them simply forgot how to laugh while sober. Even elite athletes need to mix a generous amount of humor into their lives or they may burn out prematurely.

Before my knees vetoed the idea, I was a marathon runner. Middle of the pack, I ran respectable times of under four hours for the twenty-six mile course. Once, as I participated (notice I did not say "competed") in a local marathon, I saw a distinctive couple along the race course; distinctive because the woman had her leg in a full length cast and was seated atop the hood of a sports car. Every four miles or so I spotted them. Their participant must have been a couple minutes behind me. I greeted them about mile thirteen. I waved wildly at seventeen. They picked me out at mile twenty-one. And at twenty-four, I stopped running and had a chat with them. We laughed, exchanged names, discussed knees, and as their friend came by, I joined with him and we completed the race together. Losing a few minutes was a small price to pay for the moments of friendly conversation I enjoyed with them. I took myself, my time, and the race lightly—I took my work in life seriously.

NUTRITION

A little lightheartedness will go a long way in helping you enjoy proper nutrition. Approaching your diet with a sense of humor and a little flexibility is probably better for your health than being miserable about your diet. Many people now feel more strongly about nutrition than they do religion. In Boulder, Colorado, there are individuals who refuse to associate with others because they eat red meat. I have seen the situation where a young couple broke up because she liked to salt her food and he contended she was poisoning herself. I know of parents who have been enraged at a preschool teacher who allowed her children to eat graham crackers at recess. The pursuit of nutrition with a zeal equalled only by the Inquisition is sure to do more harm than good. I believe that every nutritional plan should account for adequate supplies of chocolate, potato chips, or (not *and*) ice cream.

Dieting to achieve weight loss is usually not a laughing matter for most overweight people. Many fail in their efforts because they associate hunger with grouchiness. The diets they pursue often give them little to smile about either. So they search to find the right diet, the perfect one with "no pain and no gain." If the perfect weight loss diet existed, there would be no incentive to develop and market new diets every year. Weight loss requires you not take yourself too seriously and that you allow for generous amounts of time for good humor. Guilt during a diet does more to sabotage success than humor ever did. Always include one sinful food in a diet, make allowances for it, and enjoy your particular sinful food—be it a piece of chocolate or a bottle of beer. Your diet should have some jokes hidden in it too. (For example every Tuesday at three p.m. you may eat whatever you want providing you wear a Groucho Marx nose and glasses, and eat the food using a knife only—while seated in front of a mirror. Hard to take yourself too seriously under those circumstances.) In the long run, weight maintenance may be easier and certainly less dreary.

And a final word for you if you constantly struggle with your weight. Remember genetics. Don't blame yourself for something that is out of your control. It could just be you weren't born a whippet.

The following diet (origin unknown) is one I prescribe when individuals seem a little too up-tight. It helps them cope with stress creatively.

THE STRESS DIET

BREAKFAST
1/2 Grapefruit
1 Slice Whole Wheat Toast, dry
8 oz. Skim Milk

LUNCH
4 oz. Lean Broiled Chicken Breast
1 cup Steamed Spinach
1 cup Herbal Tea with Artificial Sweetener
1 Oreo Cookie

MID AFTERNOON SNACK
Rest of the Oreos in the Package
1 pint Rocky Road Ice Cream
1/2 jar Hot Fudge Sauce with Nuts, Cherries, and Whipped Cream

DINNER
2 loaves Garlic Bread with Cheese
1 Large Pepperoni pizza
4 12 oz cans or 1 large pitcher of Lite Beer
3 Milky Way Candy bars

LATE EVENING NEWS
1 Entire Frozen Cheesecake (eaten directly from freezer)

RULES AND RATIONALE OF STRESS DIETING

1.   If you eat something and no one sees you eat it, it has no calories.
2.   If you drink a diet cola with a candy bar, the calories in the candy bar are cancelled out by the diet soda.
3.   When you eat with someone else, calories don't count if you don't eat more than they do.
4.   Foods intended for medicinal purposes never count, e.g. hot chocolate, brandy, toast, and Sara Lee Cheesecake.
5.   If you fatten up everyone else around you, you will look thinner.
6.   Movie related foods do not have additional calories because they are part of the entire entertainment package and not part of one's personal fuel. This includes Milk Duds, Buttered Popcorn, Junior Mints, Red Hots, and Tootsie Rolls.
7.   Cookie pieces contain no calories. The process of breaking causes calorie leakage.
8.   Coatings licked off knives and spoons have no calories if you are in the process of cooking.
9.   Foods of the same color contain the same number of calories. E.g. Spinach and Pistachio ice cream, mushrooms and white chocolate. N.B.: Chocolate is a universal color and may be substituted for any other food color.

SPIRITUALITY

Every holistic prescription includes a suggestion you

110

attend to your spiritual life as you perceive it. But first, be careful not to confuse religion and spirituality. Religion is a fairly clear-cut concept, whereas spirituality is not. Religion is not the same as spirituality; it is an organized institution, with codified beliefs, intended to assist people in their spiritual journeys. It also takes care of the necessary life transitions such as birth, marriage, and death. Often individuals involve themselves deeply with a religion and never experience awe or wonder—primary indicators of spiritual experience.

Spirituality is a personal experience blended with careful thought and searing honesty. It seeks to understand what the ultimate realities are and where you fit in the scheme. Adversity is one of the principle motivations which turns people toward spiritual examination. Twelve step programs, such as Alcoholics Anonymous, all emphasize the importance of turning one's life over to a "Higher Power" as one of the first steps in dealing with severe adversity. Wisely, such programs recognize that spirituality—even more than humor—is a very individual thing and hence don't encumber their system with dogma. They let the individual work it out.

Unfortunately, religion has suffered from a grave lack of humor for centuries; ever since St Augustine and his emphasis on fall/redemption theology. Guilt and the need for "salvation" have predominated over the creation centered theology with it's sense of Original Blessing. (For more on this subject I refer you to Matthew Fox's *Original Blessing,* Bear and Co., Santa Fe, 1983.) Since spirituality has been confused with religion, it has been erroneously assumed to be devoid of humor as well. Hence, people interested in having fun or merely enjoying laughter choose to avoid all trappings of religion and turn to "sin" for satisfaction.

The church I grew up in had an eleventh commandment: "Thou shalt not laugh or play." If you did laugh or play, you were probably breaking one of the first ten. Or the flip side went: "You can do anything in life you want, providing you don't enjoy yourself." Since religion has seemed to have such a negative opinion of humor, most people have assumed spiritual growth will inevitably require them to be droll and dull as well. So they put it off till later. They would rather enjoy humor and laughter in life rather than "be religious." Maybe they will work on their spiritual life just before they die, kind of like cramming for finals.

What can be learned of humor and spirituality? It is interesting to look at spiritual giants of most religions for part of the answer to that question. When you examine them, you encounter people of warm, gentle humor—not cold austere academics. Unfortunately, cold zealots or know-it-all evangelists seem to be representative of religious practice too often. I encourage you to look deeper. Not at medieval caricatures, not at television evangelists, and not at the Ayatollah Khomeini. Look at John XXIII, Thomas Merton, the Dalai Lama, Ghandi, or even Mother Teresa. Spiritual giants are not comedians—none of them are—but all have a genuine positive sense of humor emphasizing the joy of all creation and full out belly laughter as pleasing in the sight of God. Thomas Merton, the Trappist monk who wrote prolifically and influenced a whole generation, surprised his occasional visitor by his free-wheeling humor and the permission he gave himself to laugh—even going so far as to roll on the floor and hold his sides in peals of laughter.

I was travelling with a nun once. I knew her to be a spiritual director to many people. Quiet, but genuinely warm, she chatted with me as we flew together. The flight attendant offered us extra complementary nuts since there were very few passengers on that particular flight. At first the sister took several packages, but then thought the better of it. She returned them to the attendant and winked at me. "I better not take them back to the convent, the other sisters might get peanuts envy." She played with her face, she took herself lightly, she even minced around the edges of the forbiddens. Not profane, merely playful and accepting, she modeled positive humor and mixed the three pathways into a clever one-liner.

A properly led spiritual life will have positive humor as one of the markers of its success. You can't understand the big picture and continue to take yourself too seriously. You may take your work in life very seriously, but you will realize your "self" is not the center of the universe. You may (and should) love your "self" but you will realize where it fits in the overall scheme. The relief in seeing life from the spiritual perspective frees up your tightly defended "self" and allows it to play. For you then, God may become the Creator of play and the Sustainer of the belly laugh.

RELATIONSHIP MONITORING

You are a social being. You live in relationship to a variety of people. You experience many different roles including those of parent, child, spouse, lover, friend, co-worker, and acquaintance. Each relationship has its needs and requires its share of attention. All relationships have varying degrees of attachment. Positive humor is one of the primary ways attachment is initiated and nourished.

Stress is most painful when a relationship has gone wrong. Too often some minor annoyance grows into an insurmountable problem because of neglect. Problems in relationships are like weeds in a garden. If they are removed daily when small, they don't account for much. If they grow and become massive, removing them rips out the soil and many of the garden plants as well. Relationships, like gardens, need daily attention. They need to be watered, fertilized, weeded, and protected from insect pests. The garden of relationships is nourished by love, work, time together, and positive humor. You need to make the conscious decision to nourish all of your relationships with humor at least once a week, if not more frequently.

How does someone know of your love? You can say the words, "I love you." You can spend money for gifts. You can plan activities together. And you can share your humor with one another. Loving laughter fertilizes and waters all relationships. And the other side of the metaphor is valid as well: Too much water or too much fertilizer can kill a garden. Moderation in applying humor is appropriate. Don't drown a relationship with too much humor.

BELIEF SYSTEMS

What you believe about your personal responsibility for

your mental and physical health and what you believe about the mind-body relationship will affect not only your attitudes but also your health. If you feel you have no responsibility for your health—that it's just a crap shoot—you won't get far in any holistic process. Recall the relationship between humor and responsibility as discussed earlier. Recall, for example, that humor employed as a defense for compulsive smoking may well be negative while humor used to sustain you through personal tragedy may be life saving.

You need to contemplate your beliefs—including those about humor. They form a system that hangs together but is not always logical. Some of your beliefs are consciously held and therefor tend to look logical. Others are buried within the deepest recesses of your mind and you may not be aware of them. But, both your conscious, logical beliefs and your unconscious, illogical beliefs are part of the same system. The business of self discovery should help enlighten you about those beliefs you live by; including the ones you don't want to recognize. With self understanding, you will be able to understand your use of humor, both positive and negative.

How do you gain understanding of your belief systems? Analysis (individual psychotherapy) is one way to uncover your hidden self, but it can be gruelling business. Lengthy and sometimes boring, not to mention expensive, it turns many people off. Besides, many formal schools of analysis require accepting their theory just as completely as you would embrace a religious belief (of course, the adherents call it "science").

An alternate process may get to the essentials of your belief systems, though it may fail to get at deeply hidden parts of yourself. Self-analysis can be achieved by reading self help books, listening candidly to other's opinions of you, and keeping a journal.

However you go about it, whether through self analysis or professionally assisted psychotherapy, in the process of coming to discover your unconscious beliefs, in the process of meeting your own shadow, maintain a little gentle humor with yourself. It can be depressing damn business if you don't. Self examination often degenerates into self criticism and results in guilt and finally depression. When some of my patients are in such a downward spiral, I try to let them know they are not Atilla The Hun, but rather a person like many others who was once thoughtless or mistaken—and I remind them they can make amends. Forgiveness is a very positive experience and should be followed by a sense of relief and recovery of humor. Consciously build humor into your belief systems as you examine your life. The broad definition of humor is what you need. By now, you understand it is more than jokes.

PREVENTATIVE HEALTH PRACTICES

This is the "left-over" category in the wellness concept. It includes such things as avoidance of smoking, wearing seat belts, flossing your teeth, getting pap smears, knowing your blood pressure etc. *Taking yourself lightly is not license for self neglect.* Rather it means you will take steps for your own health care with a good-natured manner. You won't groan about being three years behind on your pap smears and then avoid making an appointment. Instead you will smile to yourself, make the appointment, and stop making such a big deal of it. You will buckle your seat belt with a chuckle, rather than a cursing the dimwits who promulgated legislation making seat belt wearing mandatory. A little humor here will go a long way.

I once visited a dental hygienist who thought guilt was the best way to get me to floss. Rather than incorporating some humor in her teaching process, she seemed downright angry at me. Such behavior on her part did not make me change my flossing patterns; it motivated me to switch dental hygienists. In health care education, guilt won't work anymore. We are in a consumer oriented, marketing intensive, health care industry. A little humor will enhance the learning process and help people engage in new, more healthy behaviors. And they will return again for whatever service is needed.

To summarize, humor is not a separate dimension of the

wellness concept. It is a component of each dimension. Whether it is good natured aerobic exercise or prayer that anticipates cosmic laughter, humor adds the ingredient that helps keep you involved. Without humor, a wellness orientation to life will become dull and will probably fail. Good humor is a necessary ingredient on the way to a healthy lifestyle and then it becomes a by-product of high level wellness once you are there.

CHAPTER XII

No Snake Oil Here

The Use of Humor to Combat Illness

Inquiring minds want to know. Is it true that laughter will cure cancer? How about heart disease, acne, or maybe mild obesity? Halitosis? After Norman Cousins' remarkable experience in which he used humor as a component of self directed care, the common mind has often held the mistaken notion that humor is a cure for physical illness. Norman never suggested that. He proposed if you pursue a whole gamut of positive psychological experiences you will change your physical and psychic ecology to enhance healing. He also retained outstanding physicians and participated in appropriate, traditional medical care. He wasn't the easiest patient to care for. He checked himself out of the hospital. He questioned his caretakers and investigated a wide variety of holistic health alternatives. He didn't passively adapt to the "system" and follow medical directives like the proverbial lamb to slaughter.

There are more lessons in Norman's experience than merely humor's benefits. You need to be an informed consumer of health care. You need to enter a cooperative arrangement with your caregivers and be part of the decision making process. *Thou shalt not be passive when it comes to your own health.* When in doubt, be a little creative—bordering on wacky. Look for the lessons or messages in an illness. Put theologically: What does God or your Higher Power want you to learn from the experience? Often an illness or even an injury tells you something must change—be it a relationship, your career, or some self destructive behavior pattern.

Simple promises of cure are dangerous or at least inaccurate. The travelling medicine show promised every possible benefit from its "snake oil." But when it came down to reality, about the only thing you could count on was twenty percent alcohol, food coloring, and some weird aromatic resins. Medicine has recoiled from medical claims that are unsubstantiated. It abhors anecdotes and personal testimony. Nowadays medical science has gone overboard in the other direction. When I was in medical school some twenty-plus years ago, we knew cholesterol was important in the genesis of heart disease, but because there wasn't the final clincher—100% proof positive, without a single statistical stone left unturned—many physicians would not counsel their patients to avoid cholesterol. I would rather they had recalled Pope's couplet:

"Be not the first by whom the new are tried,
Nor yet the last to lay the old aside."

If we wait for something to be absolutely proven, we might die waiting. There is always a special interest group intent on arguing some trivial point. For example, the tobacco lobby is still trying to convince us that smoking does not lead to heart attacks and cancer. They have some well oiled statisticians and lawyers who swim fearlessly in tropical waters.

So, what's the scoop on humor curing disease? Well, *it probably won't.* I wouldn't count on it. Those who believe it will—and practice their belief—may well die laughing.

American medicine isn't perfect, but until something better comes along, I will continue to seek its help. I will continue to be a practitioner of its science and art—and psychiatry is mostly art, despite recent technology. But I will also look at a wide variety of alternative health care offerings. I confess on pain of being forever banished from the AMA, I go to a chiropractor—and she helps me. I investigate varying nutritional supplements and I will remain radically open to other possibilities. But in the process I won't thumb my nose at proven medical treatments.

Patients often turn from western allopathic medicine with the anger of a petulant child. I had two patients die of cancer of the cervix. This disease is virtually 100% curable. They refused traditional medical and surgical care in preference for laetrile and coffee enemas. Later, I had to counsel these women's children. It was tough. After all, their mothers didn't need to have died. A little humor instead of paranoia would have gone a long way in helping them accept appropriate surgery and, if necessary, chemotherapy.

So where does humor fit in dealing with physical illness? *Humor is good psychic nutrition.* Just as we need good physical nutrition to stay healthy, to combat disease, and to enhance healing, we need good psychic nutrition as well. Humor, together with the host of positive human emotions, nourishes our psyches and indeed our very souls. Our psyches, our souls, and our bodies are part of an interdependent complex that makes up the being that we are—they are intimately entwined. You cannot affect one without affecting the others. And a word of caution is in order: Just as too much of one nutrient may lead to malnutrition and too much of certain vitamins (vitamin A for example) may be fatal, so also too much humor may be damaging. Humor applied in the absence of the other positive emotions is not healthy and is potentially dangerous. You may deny reality and you may turn off others with your monomania.

At a workshop once, I pushed the audience to fully experience the zygomaticus progression. The crowd had a great time. After the exercise, one of the participants was laughing in pain; as he held his side, he explained he had gall bladder surgery two weeks before. He came to improve his humor thinking he would heal faster. He succeeded in popping a few of his stitches. Though funny, it was no laughing matter. I now routinely caution an audience to refrain from vigorous participation in the exercises if they have some medical problem that might be aggravated by raucous laughter. I advise them to "feel the humor more on the inside" for now and laugh more vigorously when they are physically up to it.

Many medical conditions may be aggravated temporarily by vigorous laughter. Asthma, bronchitis, recent surgery, lumbar disc disease, urinary stress incontinence, inguinal hernias, acute mania, and the list could go on and on. If necessary, you can experience humor without full laughter and avoid some risks. Holding back is safer but a bit less heartening. It does not produce the same benefits, such as endorphin release with its relief of pain and sense of well-being. Hence, only when it is physically safe, I encourage people to laugh heartily and enjoy the full blown experience.

Though I make no claims that humor will cure physical illness, *I do recommend its application in absolutely every phase of an illness* from onset, through diagnosis and treatment, to full recovery. In the early stages of an illness, be careful that humor doesn't respond to your fear and deny the illness. You may need humor to help you deal with your fear if you suspect the illness may be life threatening. For example, a man who experiences some chest pain might use humor two ways. Fear/denial: With a chuckle he comments, "You can't pay attention to every little ache and pain or you'll become a mental case." Humor to cope: "Heck, if I have a heart problem, I might get some more time to fish; I think I'll check it out." I have known many unfortunate souls who prevented early diagnosis of a truly serious illness because fear paralysed them. In their fear, they cracked a joke of sorts, and they denied anything was wrong; they lost precious time which could have been used for cure.

During diagnosis and treatment, humor is as indispensable as hope. While you wait, it keeps your spirits up. Humor will help the time pass more quickly. Positive humor will also enhance your relationships with caretakers and loved ones. All nurses know that the squeaking wheel might get the grease, but the playful patient gets the best—and longest—back rubs.

Following recovery, humor gives you something to look back upon besides pain, fear, and discomfort. After a friend had surgery on his foot, he kept the plastic urinal (he had never needed it, but the hospital made him buy it) and used it for a water pitcher for his plants. Humor is there to make the going easier. It is there for your positive psychic nutrition—and that of your fellow travellers.

One evening I was presenting a workshop at a local church. The basement meeting room was filled with folks from five to ninety-five. In the front row on the left of the center aisle sat a man with crutches and one leg. His wife and he were attentive, enthusiastic participants. About midway through the two hours, he gradually turned pale and appeared disoriented. My attention, and that of a good proportion of my audience, was drawn toward him. His wife spoke quietly to an accompanying friend and she went to the kitchen. She returned quickly with a glass of orange juice, a couple cookies, and some water. I stopped and inquired if I could be of any assistance. His wife smiled and assured me everything was under control. So the show went on and the man gradually emerged from his brief sojourn into insulin shock. At the end of the program, they were among the last to leave. The sweat drying from around his neck, he was all smiles again. His wife was grateful I didn't make more of a deal of it, and then she told me the following story.

"Fred has had unstable diabetes for years. We both believe that humor has been one of our best allies in this terrible disease. He had his leg amputated one month ago tonight. All our friends were so concerned. They kept calling: How's Fred? How's Fred? They were all so well-meaning and so serious. Finally, for my own sanity, I replied to a caller, 'Well, Fred is fine. He is eighteen pounds lighter and a foot shorter.'"

Both she and Fred laughed. Their laughter didn't deny his disease; their laughter celebrated their life, their guts, and their ability to overcome the adversity.

At seventy-six, my father was dying from cancer. Weakened and in constant pain, he needed morphine injections several times a day and spent much of his time in an eerie twilight consciousness. He had made his peace with God; he knew he was dying. I hastened across the country with my family. My youngest son, Dad's namesake, was merely nine months old. It was important for Christ J. (as he liked to be called—"The J. is for Junior. And it's Christ with a short "i"—not the same as Jesus' last name."), Christian III, and Christian IV to be together once on this earth. Christian IV was born in Florida and Dad lived in North Dakota. Dad was known for his great humor. He brightened when we arrived and asked for a pass to go home that afternoon. Together with his morphine and cane, he came home dressed in undershirt and pajama bottoms. He sat in his favorite chair and turned the fan on himself since it was a hot August afternoon. He then extracted one of his famous cigars from a leather case and lit up. (It would be a fallacy to say he smoked a cigar. Actually, he chewed it from one end and it burned from the other. Usually he met the glowing ash somewhere near the middle.) He then played with his grandsons. Not nimble, he used his cane to reach toys and entertain the boys. A wonderful interlude was had by all. For a final photograph, he held Chris on his lap and adjusted his cigar to the same side of his mouth as the pacifier that Chris chewed on. He modeled the positive use of humor during his waning days of life and left a gift of immeasurable value.

A physician who works with spinal cord injuries has assured me that the single most important factor in predicting a favorable adjustment to paraplegia or quadriplegia is not physical condition, not career, not age or gender, but rather the willingness of the patient to use humor to cope with his disability *every day*. If you ever get a chance, visit a wheel chair competition of some sort. You will be amazed to see the positive humor they all use. They laugh at their disabilities, at themselves, and at the consequences of being handicapped. They play, they compete, but they don't take themselves too seriously. For example, at a paraplegic skiing competition recently held in Colorado (paraplegics ski on toboggans of sorts), they gave the usual awards for speed and style. More importantly, they gave awards such as best "face plant," best "crash and burn," and the most coveted "Kamikaze Award." These folks have made it.

The next time you are ill, look about yourself and ask

what you can do to incorporate humor into the process. Pain and that "yukky" awful feeling are natural parts of an illness. Humor may not come spontaneously for you at such a time; it may have to be cultivated. Perhaps your efforts will consist of brief humorous vignettes or simple one liners. Don't try to make the whole illness funny or try to develop a comedy routine. See if some cartoon books appeal to you. If you have access to a VCR, try watching something that tickles your funny bone. *Let your sick bed become your laughing place as well.* The chapter on applications contains specific formulae for using all the ideas of this book in dealing with illness—both everyday illness and the life-threatening variety.

CHAPTER XIII

Bluer Than Blue

The Role of Humor in Depression

To understand the nature of light, you must also experience the reality of darkness. To appreciate the wisdom of humor, you must acknowledge the desolation of its absence. Six percent of the world population experiences a major depression at some time in their lives. The vast majority of humankind, regardless of culture or nationality, experiences a depressed mood sometime during life. "Depression" is not the same as a depressed mood. It is not only quantitatively different but qualitatively different as well. Depression is a biochemical hell filled with self loathing and hopelessness that frequently offers suicide to its victims as a merciful release. Depressed moods comprise a spectrum of several conditions of the human mind which vary from trivial to serious. When you say, "I'm depressed," you're probably not truly depressed; you are experiencing a depressed mood of one form or another. Your companions may respond with "lighten up" or "try a little humor, life isn't that bad." They want to believe that your depressed mood can be cured by engaging in a little bit of humor. Is it true? Can humor really cure or at least improve a depressed mood? How about a real depression? It stands to reason that it should help. Right?

There isn't a simple answer to the application of humor

in depressed moods and major depression. First, you need to learn the spectrum of human depressed moods and then you can see how humor applies in each one.

THE BLAHS

Popularized by a commercial slogan several years ago, the blahs are one of those depressed moods that occur in everybody's life. They are the "bad days" when you just don't feel up to your old self. You may have gotten up on the wrong side of the bed, the cat might have mistaken your new couch for the litter box, or your morning paper was thrown in the middle of your wet lawn. Everybody has a bad day now and then. Throughout history efforts have been made to understand the blahs. Biorhythms, numerology, and astrology are but a few systems which attempt to account for bad days. I won't comment on them beyond saying that they don't hold up to scientific scrutiny. But at the moment my Neptune is in retrograde and, being a Pisces, I shouldn't make any definite statements during such a celestial configuration.

Bad days happen. It is that simple. Just don't go out of your way to blame others for your bad days. Your mood is your responsibility. Maybe you deserve a bad day. If so, go for it. Let people know you are having a bad day, wear a button with some suggestive caption like "back off, dog breath". (A Viet Nam vet patient of mine would wear a t-shirt with "nuke'em till they glow.") The key is, take responsibility for your bad day; don't blame it on others. Communicate clearly that you are having a bad day, and don't take it out on others. Just immerse yourself in the blahs.

If you want to, you can break your bad day wide open. If you choose not to indulge yourself in the blahs, don't expect medicine, alcohol, or drugs to help. Purposefully choose humor. Select three or four techniques that work for you. Don't call someone who is chronically down: "I think I'll call up Ralph and talk, he usually bums me out pretty well." Rather, call someone who usually cheers you up and carry on a light nonsensical conversation with her for a while: "Nancy, I have been thinking of taking a course in basket weaving in Lima, Peru. Would you be interested in taking a trip there this evening to check it out?" Humor is *the* specific antidote for a bad day. It is your choice whether to use it. It works better than anything else.

THE BLUES

Being a stimulus for a major musical genre, the blues are those predictable sad and lonely feelings which every person feels at one time or another. Psychiatry has a diagnostic category for the blues, they are called "Situational Adjustment Reactions with Depressed Mood" (DSM III 309.00). It is normal to feel down, sad, blue, lonely and simply awful in response to certain of life's blows. Most of the time, the blues follow loss, e.g. loss of love, divorce, loss of hope, moving away of a friend or child, loss of self esteem, loss of money, or loss of a dream. It is normal to feel the blues in response to a loss. It is normal to feel down, tearful, sad, sick, and humorless.

The concept of the blues came out of a racial subculture that had lost its roots, its language, its dignity, and its family connections. It expressed the heart of a people who lost more than any people ever could loose. It came from the Blacks who were "freed" from slavery but had already lost everything. After all of their losses, what did they have? What did they keep? They kept their music and they kept their humor. Listen carefully to the blues. They do not suggest you commit suicide and disappear from the face of the earth. They cry out with anguish and then they whisper small hidden jokes and tricks to their listeners. In the midst of their oppression, Blacks created their own specific humor. Often it was so "in" to their culture that it went "over the heads" of white observers. Is it any coincidence that the two ethnic minorities which have received the most unremitting prejudice in the history of our country have populated the stage with the highest number of comedians—Blacks and Jews?

It follows that to survive the blues, humor (and music?) must be pursued and developed. Humor will not make the blue situation right. Humor will not right an injustice. But it will help the oppressed survive without giving in and without giving up.

When you are in the midst of the blues, take a break for humor. With a friend, go out of your way to experience humor and laughter. Pick out a funny movie to see—if you like Chevy Chase's movie, *Vacation*, go see it for the tenth time. Or go to a greeting card shop and browse, or buy yourself a Groucho Marx nose and glasses. Rest assured, the painful situation will be there when you get back, but you will be a little stronger when you return to face it again. And you may be less vulnerable to letting the blues develop into the black hole we call major depression.

DYSTHYMIA—A BLUE BELIEF SYSTEM

Dysthymia is a professional term psychiatry uses to describe people who are chronically blue. These are people who rarely laugh or smile. For dysthymics, the blues are a way of life. Dysthymics often become this way because they experienced painful childhoods that prohibited mirth of any kind. All forms of child abuse—verbal, physical, and sexual—virtually destroy the capacity of the developing child to experience humor with any ease.

Another form of pathology that evokes a humorless spirit like dysthymia is post traumatic stress disorder (PTSD). Combat soldiers are prone to this, but it may happen to any witness of a disaster or victim of a violent crime. Terror, especially if the event was senseless and out of the victim's control, permanently damages the mind, overshadowing it with such foreboding that it leaves little room for humor experience.

While observing comedy, dysthymic individuals smile insincere smiles while other participants are rolling around on the floor in peals of hilarity. Dysthymics do get some satisfaction out of hard work. Being serious, hard workers, they often are promoted in organizations and spread their dysthymia around. This may account for some organizations frowning on humor even when it is positive.

The mere application of humor does not treat dysthymia. Humor usually alienates the dysthymic person. The treatment of dysthymia requires professional intervention or involvement in some form of self help group, such as a twelve step program. Later on, when treatment is progressing, and a person is emerging from dysthymia, the pursuit of humor is an essential ingredient of recovery. Humor is a tool of healing as well as an end result of recovery.

GRIEF

In this context grief refers to bereavement—the process of letting go of a loved one who has died. Grief is difficult business. Our relationships with loved ones are complex; they consist of love, anger, memories (some good, some not so good), dreams, hopes, unspoken fears, secrets, etc. During life we are connected by a great psychic umbilical cord to those we love. When the loved one dies, the cord is amputated completely and forever—at least in this life. And we are left with a big stump to heal. It's big, it's raw, and it takes time to heal. Depending on the relationship, it may take a very long time.

In some families or subcultures, laughter during grieving is seen as neurotic or irreverent. For them, bereavement requires total abstinence from all forms of laughter or humor. Is this good? Does this abstinence—from humor and laughter— promote healing and the ultimate growth of the survivor, both psychologically and spiritually? I don't think so.

Growing up, I had a best friend. Throughout high school and college I treasured his friendship above all others. While I was on a camping trip in the mountains, he died in a tragic auto accident. No word made it to my wilderness location. I returned home to learn of his death and his funeral which had occurred weeks earlier. We were truly "best friends." I didn't know death could hurt so deeply. I didn't know I had so many tears in my body. I thought I might dehydrate from my crying. Then his mother called me and asked me to drop over to the house and talk to her about some of "those crazy things" Johnny and I did as teenagers. I went to her house. We hugged—a real anomaly for Scandinavian North Dakotans during the early sixties. We sat down with coffee and after some more tears, I began to tell some stories she never heard.

Once Johnny and I had been out on the plains driving her big Buick Roadmaster around when we ran out of gas. A helpful farmer allowed us to buy some of his fuel. We paid him and took our gas cans out to his fuel tanks and filled them up. We put the fuel in the Buick and started it. Unfortunately the fuel wasn't gasoline at all, it was kerosene. The car coughed and sputtered; it worked like a diesel, you couldn't turn it off if you tried. We took the key out and it just chugged and coughed but refused to stop running. We drove directly home, car lurching all the way, and parked it in their garage. Having enough sense to leave the garage doors open, we left the scene of the crime and went downtown for the rest of the afternoon. When Johnny and I returned to his home that evening, his mother asked what was wrong with the Buick. "The Buick?", we asked incredulously. Why we had no idea, we had been downtown all day. We got by with it. We never told her. No real harm came of it. The Buick ran out of kerosene before anyone figured out the problem. The next morning we filled it with gas and got by with a major blooper.

When I told her the story, we laughed and laughed. We remembered this wonderful, lovable rogue who was gentle and playful and mischievous all in one. In our laughter we remembered our love for him. In our shared laughter we expressed our grief with deep, healing honesty.

Appropriate laughter while recalling the happy times is humor's role in human grief. It is not neurotic and it is not irreverent. The use of humor in this way allows for healing and the recovery of the capacity to love again—and to laugh again.

MAJOR DEPRESSION

Empty, so cold you feel it in your teeth. Totally alone with a mind that never turns off. It never stops. It just keeps going on and on and on. It never solves anything. The empty cold silence loathes you. Nothing is good. Hope is the drivel of a fool. No one can help—nor should they. If not death, then this never ending blackness is your just reward for your deep iniquity.

A major depression is among the worst hells available to human beings in this life. I know victims of depression who have had third degree burns or broken bodies earlier in their lives. Every one of them would sooner reexperience any physical torment than live through another day of depression.

When the chemistry of the human brain becomes unbalanced, the victim may experience a depression. The causes of the abnormal chemistry are several, but among the leading causes is a genetic predisposition. Severe loss or grief may deteriorate into depression. Some drugs have been known to cause it too. Once the chemical storm is in motion, no humor on earth will touch it. It's just so much blowing in the wind. Major depression requires professional treatment usually involving the use of antidepressant drugs. Not uppers, these drugs restore the depressed mind's chemistry to normal. They do not promote a high. They have no street value. In some unremitting cases electroshock therapy is the only way out. The way it is administered nowadays is humane and often lifesaving.

I do not suggest humor for depressed individuals. I don't try to joke with them. I let them know that I understand them and that I aim to help. I will do whatever is within my skill to deliver them from their private hell. Efforts at humor make depressed people feel worse because they recognize that something should be funny and they recognize their inability to feel any gladness at all—in the process, they feel even worse.

As the treatment proceeds, however, I look for the reemergence of spontaneous humor. It is a sign of recovery. Once the patient offers his own jokes, I know recovery is right around the corner, and I start to employ humor liberally. I play with double meanings and absurdities and I let my face become more animated. I help the recovering depressive take himself a great deal more lightly than his depression allowed. Then humor becomes therapeutic.

CONCLUSION

Humor helps depressed moods. Humor has a role in the recovery from a major depression. You need to understand your particular form of depressed mood and then apply humor appropriately. If this chapter applies to someone you love, share it with him or her, and then talk. If your loved one identifies with one of the categories, you're ninety percent of the way to getting better. If major depression seems likely, get professional help. No self help book is enough to counsel a person through that nightmare without a caring professional.

CHAPTER XIV

Techniques

How to Incorporate This Book into
Daily Life

If you have just picked this book up and decided to start reading here, you are probably the kind of person who splits an Oreo Cookie, licks the frosting off and then throws the wafer parts away. Shame on you. To make use of this chapter, you need the information contained in all the preceding chapters. If you have read the whole book to this point, you now understand the broad theory of humor. You understand the relationship between behavior and perspective in the humor experience. You recognize that humor is essential to surviving adversity. You know how to make it work, i.e. relationship, rapport, setting, and timing. You can distinguish the three pathways to humor experience: Non-verbal interactions (face play and eye contact), stimulation of forbidden subjects (e.g. scatological humor) and verbal (jokes, wit, word play, and absurdities). You can tell the difference between positive and negative humor. You understand how to apply humor in a wellness lifestyle and how to use it to cope with depressed moods. You are a gelastologist and can practice the seven steps of the zygomaticus progression. And by now, you may be convinced that positive humor is one of the primary manifestations of human loving.

Now you are ready for techniques, specific tasks you

can undertake to enhance your experience of humor. This is the lab. Now you put the theory into action. Before you start, remember that practice takes time and repetition. Don't expect to bat a thousand. One out of three is good enough for the major leagues, and it should be good enough for you too. Apply these techniques for at least six weeks. Change, evidenced by more automatic humorous behaviors and an inner sense of being good-natured, will soak in gradually—you must allow some time.

FACE PLAY

The medium of nonverbal humor expression is the human face. Explore ten different humorous expressions in front of the mirror—in the privacy of your own home. Decide on the four funniest, and then use them when the setting and timing seem appropriate. Examples of faces: Blow up, suck-in, cross eyes, baby bubble blower, tongue wag, standard clown, finger manipulation of ears, eyes, nose, or mouth. Remember that your face is constantly giving feedback to your brain about the state of your feelings—it isn't just a one-way path from brain to face. Playing in this way will start to convince your brain that you may be a good deal more lighthearted than it was lead to believe.

FACE PHOTO

Get a trusted friend or—in the absence of such a person—go to your local K-Mart or similar such store. Take photographs of your four silliest faces. Keep the photos in your billfold. Then, one day, when you are taking yourself too seriously, pull them out and remind yourself that those people are you, too. You will be able to get a perspective on yourself and start taking yourself a little more lightly. Besides, it will give you something else besides dirty underwear to worry about if ever you are in an auto accident.

134

FAMILY FACE PLAY

The same principles apply as in private face play, but now the family does it together. Set time for two minute face play periods, e.g. before leaving for a movie or after dinner. Quite entertaining when the grandparents come to visit. Don't be surprised if they enter the play also. This process involves the whole family and affects everyone's humor for the better.

FAMILY FUNNY PHOTO

Now put your camera on a tripod or have a friend do the honors. Take several pictures of the family looking crazy. Pick the best, enlarge it, and place it in the hallway, on the refrigerator door, or in a prominent place at the office for all to see. Whatever has been said about families here applies to all sorts of couples and relationships as well—roommates, friends, lovers, spouses. Again, this process extends humor enhancement to the whole family. The kids will be able to see that the folks aren't quite as stodgy as they suspected. Breaking stereotypes is one of the goals of positive humor; all parents know kids have prejudices about their parents' senses of humor.

EYE CONTACT—"I" CONTACT

Humor is a communication. For it to be most effective, eye contact is essential. Not just eye contact, but pupil-of-the-eye to pupil-of-the-eye contact as if you are looking through that small window into the very soul. When humor is positive, this action results in enhanced intimacy. But when humor is negative, that look may be experienced as a piercing glance—an invasion: "He seemed to look right through me." Be good-natured and light hearted when you make eye contact. Don't try to play Dracula or Freud.

GELASTOLALIA

Memorize the seven steps of the zygomaticus progression. Know yourself well enough to know where you block your expression. Then whenever something strikes you as funny—and the setting is appropriate—always add one more step. Become an addicted gelastolologist. Try to make it to stage seven at least once a month. Consciously practice the zygomaticus progression when you are exposed to appropriate humorous stimulation. Especially practice it with a loved one when you are feeling the blues. It may help prevent the slide into depression or physical illness.

WILLING VICTIM LIST

Make a list of subjects that you are willing to be teased about. There must be at least three subjects that don't offend you; that in fact amuse you about yourself. (If that is not the case, you are a tight ass.) There may be subjects that are *verboten*, document those too. Thus, intimate others and coworkers will know what is OK for teasing and what is not. Gradually let the list increase as new subjects arise. Teasing itself should not be off limits, but it should be respectful of everybody's feelings. Teasing should only occur between consenting parties and it should go both ways. Otherwise it may become aggressive and cause increased anxiety for the victim of the teasing.

FORBIDDEN SUBJECT LIST

Do yourself a favor. List subjects, words, and body functions that are simply off limits to you. Especially in family and work settings, these lists can help clarify the boundaries of positive humor for everyone in the environment. At first, this list should be specifically written down for your own information. In relationships it is wise to share a specific list as a starting place for sharing positive humor. Perhaps, as time goes by, you will allow an off-limits word once in awhile, providing the story is truly funny. Spouses should respect one another's forbidden subject list carefully.

BLOOPERS

Recall life's most embarrassing moments (like my fly story), embellish it slightly, and then retell it. Blooper sharing is one of the surest ways to manifest taking yourself lightly. Of course a little discretion is needed here. If you once dated a sheep and were addicted to drinking Woolite, you might be wise to censor that story. Everybody has a socially acceptable blooper—and usually more than just one.

STORYTELLING

This goes beyond bloopers. These are stories that are not necessarily true, but would be a lot of fun if they were. These are tall tales. This art form has nearly disappeared from our culture. Too bad. Storytelling stimulates the imagination better than television or movies ever will precisely because it leaves room for the imagination to work. And it provides for a special relationship between storyteller and audience. Be clear when storytelling that you are purposely stretching the story a little bit here and there and then enjoy your creativity. Absurdity and exaggeration find their boldest playful expression in tall, unbelievable tales.

PROPS

Buy a few props that you feel express a character for you that seems just right. The standard Groucho Marx nose and glasses is a classic; but there are also wigs, fake noses, garish earrings, outlandish neckties, and whimsical underwear. Try small plastic children's toys or small trophies for unusual "successes." Keep your props at home, in your car, in your desk, in your purse or briefcase. Never be more than a minute away from a prop. You can break up an otherwise difficult moment by bringing out your prop when the going seems tense.

CARDS

The greeting card industry is overflowing with humorous cards of every type. They know that people have different levels of sensitivities and have created cards from the grossest forbidden to the mildest pun. Browse through and read some when you have time. They may help a blah day, even if you don't buy one. On the other hand, sending humorous cards can be really fun—and is what the card industry has in mind. Be sure you are sensitive to the recipient's forbiddens and don't violate them. For example, I wouldn't suggest sending a Christmas card to a straight-laced minister which showed the stable scene and everyone looking down in astonishment as Mary proclaims, "It's a girl." On occasion, you may want to send a card anonymously— it can be fun especially if you know the recipient will enjoy trying to figure out who sent it.

BOOKS OF CARTOONS OR JOKES

Cartoon books are particularly humorous. And there is a constant parade of short and very funny books about all sorts of subjects like *Sniglets*—any word that doesn't appear in the dictionary, but should. (My favorite sniglet is "rignition: n. The embarrassing action of trying to start one's car with the engine already running.") Other topics include Murphy's laws, or the elaboration of flatus. Select the books that amuse you. Read them with your family or friends. Cut out what amuses you the most and post it on the refrigerator or on the mirror in the bathroom. When a book gets boring to you, put it in your bathroom library. The next guest who walks out with it in hand and is laughing gets to take it home.

BOOKS—REAL ONES BY AUTHORS WHO ARE FUNNY (FEW OR NO PICTURES)

There are many funny authors. Ask your friends to see who they are reading or check out the critics choices in Sunday supplements. Borrow books from friends or the library, or better yet, go to the bookstore and buy them—after all that is how authors make a living. An example of a very funny author is Erma Bombeck. Part of what makes her so appealing is the underlying truth of family life that she caricatures. Her positive humor can help teenagers and parents find a mutual humor sharing ground. Particularly, her books are helpful for the middle aged individual in the midst of the blues.

RADIO

Radio had a great day in the forties and fifties when comedy shows like "The Jack Benny Show" were the primary form of stimulating laughter for millions of people. Alas, it is not so today. National Public Radio's "A Prairie Home Companion" went a long way to filling that void. Though Garrison Keillor headed for greener pastures, the reruns are just as funny the second time around.

TV

In general, TV has been disappointing in positive humor propagation. It has depended heavily upon stimulating sexual forbiddens to evoke laughter and it leaves too little to the imagination. Often it has failed to appeal to any altruistic values. Two shows stand out over the past decade, and they do so because they had a serious message that accompanied the humor: M*A*S*H and THE BILL COSBY SHOW. M*A*S*H clearly spoke to the senselessness of war and COSBY to the trials of parenthood which we all go through. The use of humor in adversity shows how positive humor assists survival during war or raising teenagers.

COMEDY STORES AND NIGHTCLUBS

These places do entertain a specific audience. They rely on alcohol and liberal transgression of forbidden subjects, usually sexual, drug related, or ethnic. Such settings are probably fine for some folks since they provide a place where they can loosen up and experience some laughter. But more often, they are offensive to the majority of the population.

YOUR OWN ACCENT, CHARACTER, OR CLOWN

This is primarily for extroverts. Develop an ethnic accent preferably one of your own ethnic origin, or develop several if you have the skill. If you feel theatrical, develop a character who is a little outlandish. Let her out to play once in a while. Clowning can be fun, but is often serious business since finding the clown within you is a psychotherapeutic process requiring considerable introspection.

MIME

Learn some simple mime maneuvers. You don't have to do them well. But mime delights kids and adults as well. You only have to try three or four such tricks. Go to a mime workshop and pick up a few ideas for yourself and play with them.

JOKES

Finally the subject that most people associate with humor. Purposely I left it to the end of the list. If you want to be a joke teller, you must find some sources of material and write the jokes down just as you would do homework. The jokes need to be consistent with the person you are, your persona. Whenever you hear one you like, write it down. When you have a collection, learn them well enough that you can tell the jokes from memory.

Never tell them verbatim. Tell them in your own words with your own pauses and change them to fit your own settings and characters if necessary. Give sufficient time for suspense to build in the listener's imagination before you hit the punch line. Never laugh louder than your audience; if anything downplay your own laughter, but make eye contact with a whimsical, playful—but not self-satisfied—smile. Keep ten punch lines in your billfold at all times and rotate them once a month, just to keep your material fresh.

GIVE THIS BOOK TO A FRIEND OR LOVED ONE

Then you both will be coming from the same frame of reference. In fact, if several people read this book, they can join together for a form of humor support group. Such a group meets about four times for an hour or so and shares what was the most helpful guide to personal change that each received from the book—no therapy please. Then share a blooper, a story, a prop, and a joke. Think how well this would work if the support group were your family or your coworkers, as well as your friends.

TWELVE POSITIVE HUMOR AFFIRMATIONS

Affirmations are not high powered psychotherapy tools that evoke deep enduring personality change, but they are inspirational and they do serve as devices to remind you of deeper change that is important to you. The following are affirmations that express the ideals of positive humor.

1. I am determined to use my humor for positive, loving purposes only.

2. I will take myself lightly, even though I take my work in life seriously.

3. I will not seek to be offended. When in doubt, I choose to see

others as meaning well. I will practice positive paranoia.

4.   I will express my laughter physically and freely.

5.   I refuse to use my humor to express anger or prejudice; I will express negative feelings directly without contaminating my positive use of humor.

6.   I understand that the gift of laughter is a loving gift. I will laugh generously at others' attempts at humor.

7.   All teasing and ethnic humor will be by mutual consent and will go both ways, or I will not engage in such humor.

8.   I will respect the forbiddens of my companions in life and I will enjoy my own use of forbidden subjects freely and without guilt.

9.   If I offend another by my use of humor, I will make amends.

10.   I will be eternally vigilant for the jokes and absurdities of the universe. I will go out of my way to share my observations with my companions in life.

11.   In adversity I will use humor to cope, to survive, and to grow.

12.   On the day of my death I will look back and know that I laughed fully and well.

Applications

*How to Use the Techniques in
Specific Life Circumstances*

This is the final step. Beyond theory. Beyond ex-
planation. Beyond distinction and admonition. Here are the
systematic applications of the theory and techniques. Now you
can make this material work for you—in real life, your life.

The questions people ask about humor are so diverse
and yet so much the same:

"Are there simple day-to-day applications anyone can
use?"

"Can I *really* change my sense of humor?"

"I am married to a wonderful man, but he doesn't have
any sense of humor at all—how can I help him to lighten up?"

"I work in a pressure cooker. Nobody laughs. Can I
really help to change the tone?"

"How can I handle difficult people with humor?"

"My brother has cancer—do you think humor can help?
Will it help him survive?"

"My friend's teenage son just committed suicide—how
can humor help?"

"Where does humor fit into rejection or other life
traps?"

"I'm unemployed, I'm fifty-one, and I don't have a skill

anybody wants—how should I laugh my way out of this?"
"My nephew is quadriplegic....."
Etc., etc., etc.

More questions exist than answers. Human adversities are too numerous to count. I cannot answer each question in a completely satisfactory way. But I can answer in general. The following are formulae to follow as you use humor to combat life's adversity.

TO IMPROVE YOUR OWN SENSE OF HUMOR

1. Read the book as if it were a textbook, not a novel.
2. Memorize the zygomaticus progression.
3. Pick out four techniques (at least) and practice them daily.
4. Read the twelve humor affirmations every week for six weeks.   Spend at least five minutes in silence after reading them to let them soak in.
5. Tell two close friends you are attempting to improve your sense of humor. Ask for their feedback over the next six weeks.
6. After week two, write yourself a letter explaining how you will know you have changed your humor for the better. Seal it and open it in six months (months, not weeks).
7. Review the blues chapter. Get professional help if indicated.

TO IMPROVE THE HUMOR OF (AND WITH)
A LOVED ONE

1. Give him this book as a gift. But make sure you have read it first. Avoid the tendency to underline what you think he should pay attention to.
2. Gently encourage him to read it if he seems reluctant. Spend time reading it in his presence, whet his interest like Tom Sawyer did in the whitewashing of the fence. Ideally, each of you should read it during the same general time period.
3. Make a "positive humor contract" with your loved one to

undertake systematic humor change over the next six weeks. Write it out, do not exceed a page. Include "willing victim lists" as part of the contract.

4. Memorize and practice the zygomaticus progression together.

5. Promise one another you will make eye contact when you next experience spontaneous laughter in each other's presence; commit yourselves to adding one more step of gelastolalia.

6. Select four techniques to practice; in particular, buy some props and take a funny photograph of yourselves.

7. Post the twelve positive humor affirmations on the front of the refrigerator or the bathroom mirror—wherever they can be read daily. Then, once a week, read the twelve positive affirmations aloud together and then sit in silence together for ten minutes. Avoid music or speaking at the time, just experience the silence and the intention behind the affirmations.

8. If you are lovers, consider joking and laughter during lovemaking. If you have not already chosen pet names for sexual anatomical parts or types of lovemaking, consider doing so.

9. After six weeks, take an evening to discuss whether your positive humor efforts were a success. If they were, try it again in a few months. If they weren't, would you like to give it one more chance?

TO IMPROVE THE HUMOR OF (AND WITH) A FRIEND
(Someone who is more than an acquaintance and less than "a loved one")

1. Read this book and then give it to your friend.

2. Encourage him to read it. If he doesn't read it after three efforts on your part, you will have to settle for modelling your own improved humor to influence him.

3. If he does read it, take some time and talk about it. See whether you can agree to practice some of the techniques. Be specific about what you will try.

4. Especially engage in blooper swapping and storytelling.

5. Agree on a shared private forbidden list. It is usually more

raunchy than your generic forbidden list.

6.   Agree to come to the aid of one another on blue days. If you both are having a blue day and need support, flip a coin to see who gets to stay blue and who will become the humor supporter.

7.   Agree to send two unsigned humorous cards to one another every year—but never on a special occasion.

8.   Determine whether you want to engage in an exchange of practical jokes. They are prone to negative complications, so be careful. But when practical jokes are decided upon, they are the most fun between mutually consenting adult friends.

HUMOR WITH CHILDREN—PRE TEENAGERS

1.   Read the book, but don't expect them to read it.

2.   Consciously commit yourself to sixty-seven percent "yeses" in response to their attempts at humor. Do your best to find something—anything—remotely amusing in their efforts and laugh with them. Redirect their use of forbiddens of which you disapprove. Be clear with yourself and your children when defining forbidden boundaries.

3.   Shop for favorite cartoon books, clip out your favorites, and place them on the refrigerator. Don't let one stay up too long, it tends to get stale.

4.   When your children truly tickle your funny bone, remember the zygomaticus progression and add one more step. And remember to make eye contact with them.

5.   Buy props and photograph the family in the craziest of situations. Include these in your wallet. Send them along with Christmas cards to your relatives or to Miss Manners.

6.   Gently, but consistently teach your child the difference between positive and negative humor.

7.   Intervene and explain when you observe children using humor in a cruel way. Teach empathy and ask if they can laugh just as vigorously in a positive way.

8.   Remember that joking is language dependent; what is funny to a five year old isn't to you and vice versa. Absurdities may be

the easiest form of jokes that make you both laugh.

9.   Allow your children to tease you. Exchange willing victim lists with your children—that means they can tease you too. Use this exercise as an opportunity to explain the importance of setting and timing, so they know when and where teasing is appropriate.

10.   Place the humor affirmations in a prominent place so the children have the ideas in their environment all the time.

HUMOR WITH CHILDREN—TEENAGERS

1.   Accept the fact that no matter how hard you try, no matter how sincere your efforts, and no matter how consistent you attempt to be, your teenager may find fault with this process and you will probably feel like a failure.

2.   Read the book and then decide if it is worth even trying to teach your teenager or whether you will use the information for your survival only.

NOTE: If you decide to take a chance and share humor with your teenager, continue on and good luck. If you decide not to try, continue improving your own sense of humor—work for a Ph.D. in gelastolalia. And remember not to laugh *at* your teenager. When the opportunity arises, see if you can discuss this idea of positive humor—without defensiveness on either of your parts. Then perhaps you will give it a try anyway.

3.   See whether your teenager might be interested in reading the book. You have it half way made if he agrees to.

4.   Be careful with the zygomaticus progression with teenagers, they may die of terminal embarrassment seeing their parents acting so......well....."juvenile."

5.   Try shopping for props and taking funny family photos, but let the kids have right of censorship. Above all, don't get angry when they refuse to show the pictures to anyone. After all, its the thought that counts, right? Put the pictures in a shoe box and show them to the kids when they turn twenty-five.

6.   Cartoon books are a good idea; shop for them together and choose your favorites. Clip and post them.

7.   Some TV shows work for families. M*A*S*H and COSBY seem to work the best. See whether you can agree on one funny show a week. During this time take the opportunity to apply the zygomaticus progression.

8.   When teenagers bring home "black market" humor, listen, laugh, establish rapport, and then preach later. Always remember that rule with teenagers: Establish rapport first, preach second. Formal talks on positive and negative humor are in order at this time.

9.   Alcohol, humor, and teenagers: Always affirm their right to have fun. Challenge them to have fun without requiring alcohol to do so. Model that behavior for them as well.

10.   Post the humor affirmations somewhere in the house where you know they won't be ignored.

HUMOR WITH THE ELDERLY

1.   Remember that aging changes the humor experience; it gradually disappears in the reverse order of its acquisition. But only the most senile or brain damaged have no sense of humor. Even then, can we be sure?

2.   Agree to the principle that all elderly persons have the right to experience some kind of humor—tickling the forbiddens included. Don't depend on jokes to evoke the same response as in younger adults.

3.   If the elderly person still has the capacity to read and comprehend, give this book to him or read it to him.

4.   Encourage storytelling. There is a great wealth of humorous material stored away in those aging cerebrums. Try to tap it. Use a tape recorder, get the stories right.

5.   When communicating, get close and make eye contact. Use your face as a medium of humor communication.

6.   Expect repetition. Even if you have heard the story before, it's the loving listening that counts.

HUMOR IN LIFE-THREATENING ILLNESS

IF SOMEONE YOU KNOW IS ILL:
1.   Read the book and buy a copy as a gift for the person who is ill. After a couple weeks, ask him what he thought of it. If he hasn't read it, gently suggest that it might help. But then don't push it. Every person has a right to go about handling a life-threatening illness in his own way. Because humor worked for Norman Cousins is no guarantee it will work for anybody else.

IF YOU ARE THE ILL PERSON
1.   If you have read this far, good for you. If you have not read the whole book, please do so, then you won't let any misconceptions get in your way. Become familiar with the three pathways and the theory of humor's role in dealing with adversity. (No claim is being made that humor alone will cure your illness.) Humor is an adjunctive medicine of great value; use it with all the other treatments prescribed for you.
2.   Learn the zygomaticus progression thoroughly and practice adding one more step whenever possible. If you are really down or in pain, it may mean just smiling with your whole face. That's OK for now, just add one more step whenever you can.
3.   Look about you at the people in your life. Who do you want to have around you to laugh with? Give them this book and tell them what you're doing. Then schedule times with them for storytelling and reminiscence. Perhaps watch some movies that are especially amusing to each of you. These people are your humor allies—they are your psychological T-lymphocytes. Nourish them and nurture them.
4.   Allow yourself to laugh at death—that is, when you see the cosmic humor in the process. Allow yourself to laugh about death. It will help you avoid denying its reality. After all, we all will die; the only question is when. Denial is not a good coping strategy. Humor is.
5.   Make it a goal to get your doctor to loosen up. Try something crazy like getting her a get-well card or decorating your body with a magic marker prior to a physical. Anything crazy to lighten up the doctor/patient relationship will enhance the health of both.

(We all know M.D.s need better senses of humor.)

6. Make sure your family and loved ones know you have elected to use humor to cope with and, if possible, overcome your life-threatening illness.

7. Accept the blues. You can't go through this process with a smile all the time. When you feel blue, go for it. Your laughing companions should be crying and swearing companions too. Accept that humor is not a panacea. It is a component of your will to live. Do whatever is medically appropriate and extend yourself to whatever alternative healing you believe in.

8. Remember that positive humor and spiritual growth are not only compatible, but in many cases inseparable. Your laughter does not mean irreverence about the ultimate meaning of life—it affirms it.

9. If you have a disability, is there any way you can joke about it? Be careful with this one. Don't joke about your disability until you have accepted it. Humor in the face of a disability may be the single best predictor of optimal outcome. Disability is not only a wise teacher for the disabled but is even a wiser teacher for the able-bodied who are open to its lessons.

10. Share this book with some other person who is in your shoes. In particular when you feel you have benefitted from the use of humor, become a disciple and spread the news that it is possible to use positive humor in the face of life threatening illness or disability. As long as the humor is positive, it is guaranteed to do no harm.

11. Consider starting a humor support group. Meet four times for at least an hour to share the book, props, stories, bloopers, and jokes. End the group by repeating the twelve affirmations of positive humor.

HUMOR IN BEREAVEMENT

1. *Do not* give this book to some person who is in the early stages of the grief process.

2. Humor and laughter at the recollection of the loved one need to take place within small groups who understand that laughter

during grief is part of the process.

3.   *Do* give this book to someone who has spent over six months in the grief process and still seems to be in significant pain.

4.   If possible, make sure that hospice workers and nurses who work with the terminally ill get a copy of this book as a gift. They already know how to apply it. After all, many of the concepts in this book came from them.

HUMOR FOR PSYCHIATRIC PATIENTS

This is almost too broad a subject because of the variety of disorders which may require psychiatric intervention.   In general, I would avoid giving this book to any person in crisis and I would avoid applying humor until he is showing definite signs of recovery.   Maybe the book could serve as a thoughtful gift when he is "out of the woods." But, early in the process, there is no telling how your attempts at humor might be interpreted—or misinterpreted.

If the individual is a close friend, wait until improvement is clearly evident, and then go about using this material as you would with any other friend whose experience of humor you would like to enhance.

HUMOR FOR THERAPISTS

1.   Read this book. Keep it as a reference.

2.   Learn, practice, and preach the distinction of positive and negative humor.

3.   A topic for group therapy might include how humor has affected each member in positive and negative ways.

4.   Confront negative humor and challenge the individual to use positive humor instead.

5.   Post the positive humor affirmations in a prominent place so all can refer to them as necessary. Or make up note cards with the affirmations so they can be carried on the person.

6.   Remember that humor during the early phases of a serious

mental disorder is almost always a denial of a problem or an evasion of anxiety. Humor in the later stages of therapy represents insight and positive coping style. It is up to the experienced therapist to distinguish which is which.

HUMOR IN THE WORK PLACE

(Somehow it seemed most appropriate to include this material after the psychiatric information.)

1.   Remember the principle: The amount of humor and its quality is directly related to management. If the boss laughs, everybody laughs. If the boss is neurotic, the organization will be neurotic too.
2.   Negative humor will disrupt the work place one hundred percent of the time. Positive humor is correlated with creativity and high level wellness.
3.   It follows that the pursuit of positive humor should be a high priority of any successful business.
4.   Management needs to read the book and then pass it down through their subordinates. Special emphasis needs to be added to the distinction of positive from negative humor.
5.   Positive humor should be rewarded, e.g. the joke, cartoon, or blooper of the month should be noted in the company paper or honored with a spot on a bulletin board.
6.   Negative humor needs to be identified—clearly and verbally—and then ignored. No inquisitions, please. If it persists in one individual, it should be dealt with specifically by that person's supervisor. In particular, sarcasm in the work place (and in most other places for that matter) is deadly. Identify it for what it is, "That   statement is sarcastic, please refrain from sarcasm, it offends me."
7.   The positive humor affirmations should be posted.
8.   Coffee break groups should plan for four sessions of mutual humor support rituals. If they work, then try them again in a couple months.
9.   Conduct funny prop competitions on special holidays—

everybody needs to participate; super bowl days, labor day, and the birthday of William Henry Harrison are a few examples of such notable holidays.

10.   Consider ethnic jokes about Sumerians only—after all, there are no Sumerians left on earth. Then you can start an ethnic joke with: "There were these two Sumerians, Swen and Ole..."

11.   Management needs to remember that humor is essential to cope and grow through change and adversity. It should not be prohibited, it only needs to be regulated.

"BLACK HOLE" PEOPLE

Black hole people are those negative, humorless individuals who seem to suck humor out of any environment. Like black holes in space, they are so heavy that not even light can escape from them.

1.   Black hole people need love, too. So even if they don't smile back, use your best smiles and laughs in their presence.

2.   Give them this book as a gift. No preachy inscriptions, please.

3.   Don't expect them to change immediately. Give them time, just expose them to your best—but gentle—efforts at humor.

4.   See that they get a copy of the twelve positive humor affirmations.

5.   When they have birthdays, give them gifts that have some real humor value. Pay attention to their forbiddens and don't transgress them (very far).

6.   When they are in particularly bad moods, give them space. Definitely avoid the advice to "lighten up."

7.   When they make efforts at humor, respond with the most laughter you can genuinely muster—remember the zygomaticus progression and add one more step.

8.   Assess whether they may be truly depressed. Reread the chapter on depression if you have a question. If you suspect them to be depressed, suggest—in the most confidential and caring manner possible—that they get some help for themselves.

ETC. ETC. ETC.

If there are conditions you think haven't been addressed, use your creativity. Identify the problem, see how you understand it, and then refer to the technique chapter. Set up your own application plan for the particular condition. Be ready to modify it if you get new information. Continue the applications for at least six weeks. It takes that long for behaviors to become familiar and feel like "self."

CHAPTER XVI

Of War and Peace

*The Importance of Humor
in Peacemaking*

Comradery and wonderful good times are the rule in military aviation. As a flight surgeon, I was part-time crew member, confidant, priest, drinking buddy, and family doctor to my squadron and their families. We flew the A-6A, Intruder, a medium attack bomber that could fly in all weather and—whenever all systems were working—could supposedly drop bombs with pinpoint accuracy by using radar and a fancy computer. We often travelled around the country to "visit" different bombing ranges. On one particular occasion, we were in Puerto Rico working the range on the nearby island of Vieques.

At the end of one typical good day, we were in the officers' club insuring we didn't develop an alcohol deficiency. My Marine squadron met up with a Navy fighter squadron (Squids) and challenged them to some heavy drinking. Somehow I was matched against their flight surgeon and won a contest of sorts. As winner, I was awarded to the Executive Officer (XO) of the Navy squadron to be his RIO the following day—fly second seat in his F-4, Phantom.

It sounded good to me; I had never been through the sound barrier. The F-4 was like a sleek sports car next to the truck-like A-6. I looked forward to a super good time.

When we first arrived in Puerto Rico, we had been warned to be careful about one potential problem. The Russians had just sailed eight destroyers into the Caribbean and were within a couple hundred miles of Puerto Rico. "Don't mess with the Ruskies. Leave them alone and don't cause any sort of incident." Being Marines, we never had to be told twice.

However, the morning after the officers' club contest, I was flying with Squids. We went out and flew a few "intercepts"—maneuvers in which we encountered each other as "bogeys" and then wrangled for position to shoot one another down. We played between tall cotton canyon walls and rolled the sun and sea around our canopy. The multiplied forces of gravity distorted our faces and narrowed our visual fields to pinpoints. With crisp sunlight defining every feature, we played tag like grown children frolicking through the heavens with little regard for life or gravity. It was better fun than a thousand Disneylands. Then the XO and I broke off from the flight and climbed up to the dark blue regions where the stars faintly shine. Rolling inverted, we pointed the nose back to earth and watched as the air speed eased through Mach One—no thunder clap, only a strange intense sound of air molecules polishing the windscreen. Our airspeed climbed steadily as we plummeted earthward to over a thousand miles per hour. Fast, really fast.

About then I heard a "beep" over the headphones indicating we were being "painted" by radar. In a few moments, several radars were examining us. And then came a steady tone as the radars "locked on" our Phantom. We levelled out about five hundred feet "above the deck," still flying inverted. By looking "up" through the top of the canopy, I saw the seascape stretched over my head. And there, scattered at random intervals, were several ships....Russian ships. "Hang on, Doc. They won't lay a glove on us."

We shot through the Russian flotilla with a thunderous sonic boom following on our tail. "We blew 'em off the fantails, Doc."

With that, the XO hit afterburners and pointed the Phantom to the sun. Rolling as we climbed, air bubbled out of our middle ears, and the cockpit cooled rapidly. Gradually, the radars

156

released us and we once again gamboled through the heavens. Two grown boys playing and laughing. What a kick.

"By the way, Doc, you didn't see anything happen. We were no where near the Russian fleet."

"No, Sir. No ships. Just one hell of a good ride."

Twenty years, Viet Nam, and a radical mind shift away, I speak with fellow doctors who are members of Physicians for Social Responsibility. We discuss how to present information to our communities regarding nuclear war. We need to get the word out. A nuclear holocaust is not survivable by anyone, not even "the winner." We talk of writing letters, holding meetings, giving speeches, or even trying civil disobedience. We don't seem to laugh much in our small meetings. We don't drink, party, or thump each other on the back. Things are serious. And somehow I feel something is missing. I miss the closeness and play of comrades in arms.

I talk with my fellow Quakers about rational ways to stop using war to settle disputes—after all, military victory only proves who is stronger, not who is right. We discuss writing articles, giving speeches, and trying civil disobedience. Sober, serious, and thorough, we toil through "peace with justice" concerns until consensus is achieved. Quakers are not exactly a wild and crazy group.

In this crazy national debate about peacemaking, I often feel impotent to influence anyone. The hawks already have their minds made up—they are not apt to budge. The doves, intent on peaceful solutions often seem naive. The people I need to convince, the many young people who haven't taken a stand, live for today and give little thought to Armageddon. Growing up with the sword of Damocles over their heads, they see nuclear war as some benign fixture of the times. As mythical as Camelot, the end of humankind is brushed aside in the young people's quest for amusing diversions—another party, another rock concert.

Unfortunately, apathy isn't limited to the young. I hold a meeting honoring some physicians who have travelled to the Soviet Union. They have slides and a presentation about Soviet doctors who are seeking to educate their leaders about the dangers of nuclear war. Four people show up—none of them M.D.s. I had invited three hundred people, mostly physicians.

I talk with teenagers about waging peace and they yawn. So then I talk with them about flying A-6's, dropping napalm, and air combat maneuvering. I talk about wild partying, crazy antics, and laughable good times. They hang on every word.

War is hell. Everybody agrees. No combat veteran in his right mind ever wants to return to war. It is a sad, but true, observation: *Preparing for war is a lot more fun than preparing for peace.* War's garments are sewn with the silken threads of excitement and humor. We hear told and retold stories of war and preparations for war. Viet Nam documentaries and mythical Rambo characters stimulate the vicarious need to experience war in some fashion. Excitement and humor walk hand-in-hand with warriors as they approach battle. Even documentaries—as moving as their message may be—show, interspersed with scenes of gunfire and death, GIs at play and laughing.

Recognizing this, I believe we must involve humor in our preparations for peace. Those of us who want to influence our world away from war need to practice positive humor. Not sarcasm, irony, or satire; those aggressive tactics often polarize a community and frequently become precursors to future conflicts. The verbal aggression of negative humor makes enemies of the very people we want to convert. Calling dedicated soldiers "baby killers" only makes them withdrawn, hardened, and bitter. Describing conservatives as "fascists" only moves them to further close their ears to meaningful dialogue.

We humans have to tame the excitement *and fun* of preparing for war if we are ever to create a lasting peace. No more parades and laughter to send Johnny off to fight. We have an aggressive streak and we have an adrenalin addicted streak. Neither is wholly bad, but humor has been incorporated into each in order to deny the pain that might result. It is time humor be recognized when applied negatively. Such humor should not conceal our aggression or deny our addictions.

As part of teaching peace, we must teach positive

humor. Preparations for peace need to be full, rich, and playful. Peacemaker's humor needs to play with some forbiddens as well. Laughing at themselves will go further than satirizing their opponents. Peacemakers must avoid too much piety and unconventionality. (I never understood how failing to bathe or groom oneself was supposed to influence others away from war—it actually influences others to stand up wind.) Peacemakers need to experiment with positive and effective humor practices that succeed in influencing those who disagree with them. They need to avoid coming across as naive fault finders, like the woman I met at a demonstration who saw no problem with the Russians shooting down the Korean airliner. She "knew" the CIA was at fault somewhere. When I suggested the Russians may be paranoid and aggressive too, she responded with anger.

A wonderful sixty year old woman once came to me asking how to incorporate humor into her peace activism. She had elected to violate the Nevada Test Site by hiking in on the Winter Solstice. (Big threat to our nation's security—an unaccompanied older woman with a sleeping bag and water bottle.) She knew full well she was violating a federal law and committing a felony in the process. She wanted me to teach her how to come across to the media with the success of Ronald Reagan. She didn't want to be pictured "soft in the head" or so heavenly-minded that she was no earthly-good. She wanted to be seen as good natured and clear thinking. We discussed the use of facial expression, the importance of eye contact, and the concept of taking oneself lightly. We reviewed the whole theory and practice of positive humor and effective communication.

Later, after her arrest and conviction (she received a suspended sentence provided she not commit any more felonies), she spoke warmly of knowing her stance was made more credible by her use of positive humor. Her eyes twinkled at her captors and she even quipped with her military guards. Her only regret was the media didn't make much of the event. Her impact was limited to those who actually saw her. No TV coverage—too bad since she was prepared with Reagan-like one-liners. But most importantly, she said her humor made the greatest difference to her. She believed in the rightness of what she did and had a jolly good time in the process.

I have a dream. One day I will present a positive humor workshop to the arms negotiators in Geneva. They probably need some sort of entertainment after a long day at the conference table. Educated, serious, and well intentioned, they must uphold the propaganda stance of their leaders, rather than getting down to the business of making peace. I want to tell them about my broken fly. I want them to learn the zygomaticus progression and gelastolalia. (Can you imagine diplomats making a clown face and then looking one-another right in the eye?) I want to be sure they know what positive humor is. I want them to acknowledge that all peoples want not only freedom from fear, hunger, and disease—they want the freedom to laugh, to love, and to enjoy loving laughter with their families and friends. Properly applied, justice will always foster positive humor. And conversely, positive humor will always promote justice. I hope they will know that such talk of love and laughter isn't just the ranting of a clown.

Then again, maybe I am a clown, a jester. In medieval times the jester served an important function. He made the king laugh at himself. He lightened the otherwise heavy tone. He made the king remember he was a man like everyone else, experiencing the failings and frailties of the human condition. The jester helped the king preserve his sanity and his humanity. I think I should like to be a fool for peace.

CHAPTER XVII

Job's Laughter

Beyond a Psychology of Humor—
A Very Personal Perspective

W hen it comes to explor-
ing the unknown re-
cesses of your mind, imagination may be more important than
intelligence. The creative imagination provides you with myth,
insight, and poetic expression of otherwise ineffable realities. As
I pondered adversity, the biblical character Job continued to
nudge me and insisted we talk. So I reread the story of Job and
prepared to meet him for a conversation.

You may recall Job. He was a righteous man, wealthy
and successful. Not Jewish, he actually came from a country
called Edom, but the account was written some time later by a
Hebrew writer. Satan convinced God to pour adversity upon Job
in order to test him. God allowed it, but would not let Job lose his
life. First of all—in an unbelievable variety of simultaneous
calamities—his children, servants, and animals were killed. Only
the messengers survived to bring the horrible news to Job. But
Job didn't curse God. Next Satan plagued him with ulcers from
head to foot. Job took his place on a pile of ashes, probably
feeling very depressed, but still did not curse God for inflicting
these horrors upon him.

Job's suffering attracted three amateur theologians who
visited the agonized man and developed arguments to explain his

condition. All three claimed Job had suffered because he had sinned. They felt sympathy for their tormented companion, but they were steadfast in their arguments. Job protested his innocence and groped in the darkness for a solution. None came. Instead, a new character named Elihu showed up and he continued many of the same arguments, with occasional attempts to vindicate God. Finally God had enough of this theological bull session and told them all to shut up. Speaking from a whirlwind, God informed Job and his companions that no man is a judge for God and *that's that*. Job repented of even questioning God. God rebuked the three companions and then went on to restore all of Job's wealth and friends. God even blessed him with seven more sons and three more daughters. Job lived to a hundred and forty and died a wealthy, respected, and happy man.

One quiet evening, I sat alone in front of my fireplace and prepared to have a conversation with Job. I relaxed, closed my eyes, and let the story play itself out in my imagination. I just observed, really; it took on a life of its own.

The story which came to me was unexpected. I found myself on a vast prairie of western North Dakota. Night was falling. Alone and tired, I unpacked my camping gear and went to sleep. Shortly, I was awakened; surrounded by a herd of sheep, baaing and nudging each other as they avoided tramping on my sleeping bag. In the distance, a Ford pickup towing an Airstream trailer pulled up to the edge of the sheep herd. A couple got out of the truck and entered the trailer. Soon I heard Pachelbel's *Canon in D* drifting across the prairie. Pretty unlikely set up for a shepherd. I roused myself and made my way through the sheep to the trailer. An older, Jewish-looking man dressed in Levi's and a plaid shirt greeted me at the door. He had scars scattered about his arms and face, suggesting a healed skin disease. The woman accompanying him had the relaxed figure of a comfortable older woman, her face wreathed in smiling wrinkles. I estimated them to be in their late fifties.

"Come in, Chris, we've been expecting you. I'm Job, this is my wife, Turtledove. I call her Dove for short. Would you like some tea? Or perhaps some brandy?"

A bit off balance, I opted for the brandy.

We sat down at the table and I came face to face with a warm, jolly man. Job was a bit overweight and balding slightly. His dark brown eyes smiled with the warmth of bright sunshine. The healed scars and deeply ridged crow's feet gave an earthen texture to his expressive face. He wore a green baseball cap advertising, in yellow letters, some kind of hybrid corn. Dove, dressed in a sweatshirt and denims, likewise appeared warm and accepting—very comfortable to be with.

I felt I was visiting my favorite uncle, and being treated as a grown-up even though I hadn't yet turned twenty-one. Dove rested her elbows on the table, holding a cup of herbal tea in both hands. Job leaned back in his chair, one big hand around a chipped souvenir cup, the other arm stretched along the back of the next chair. Both took their time to speak; neither acted very "heavy" (or holy) as we talked. When Job changed his position, as he often did to make a point, he would readjust his cap, or take it off and smooth his hair down and put the cap on again.

"Chris, the Hebrew who wrote my story left out a big part when he reported my life. The tragedies happened just like he said, all on the same day....Talk about your bad days. And the dialogues and the whirlwind happened too, pretty much as described. What was glossed over occurred at the end of the story. God didn't give back my friends and fortune by magic. They came back when I regained my will to live *and my sense of humor*.

"Dove's aunt was most helpful. She showed up when everybody else had about given up on me. She took me under her wing and changed everything."

Mimicking a Jewish mother, Job quoted the older woman, "'Job, you're a mess. Just look at you. Rags, sores, ashes, and all. All that talking was necessary, I guess, but now it's time to get on with life and take care of yourself. What do you say we clean you up, fix you something to eat, and then—maybe tonight when it's cooler—we can take a walk in the desert?'

"So she washed my sores and made me put on some clean clothes. She fed me Chicken Soup, her own original recipe. And later in the evening, the two of us went walking to enjoy the cool night air. We drank in the fragrance of the desert, listened to the jackals howl, and watched the stars fill the canopy of the night sky. We chatted about small things, especially the happy recollections of shared family memories. I began to relax as I remembered the wonderful—and often funny—things my children used to do. Running, laughing, playing....They would even interrupt a business meeting with some of their games—baby goats and lambs dressed up like people about to be married; things like that.....And I let them play and laugh. I think that is part of why I was so successful. I remembered many moments of shared laughter with my family and then, to my utter surprise, as I reminisced.....I smiled.....and then *I laughed*. Can you imagine that, Chris? Me, Job, the archetypal suffering righteous man, the patient one of all history? I laughed. And when I laughed, I remembered what it felt like to be alive. I remembered I still had the capacity to love. As I laughed, I recovered my will to live and carry on—even if I didn't know all the answers to the meaning of life....and knew I never would."

Job paused, looked down at his cup, and spoke with a faint smile, "For many evenings, the two of us walked together trading stories and laughing with ease. About the same time, my friends returned to talk about village affairs and even began to transact business with me. I think they were attracted by my sense of humor. Certainly they weren't attracted by my indomitable patience or my tragic life history. I could take myself lightly and this reassured them."

Job put his cup aside and reached for Dove's hand. They looked at one another and then back to me. "I returned with my newfound hope and humor and decided to spend more time with Dove. Deep inside, I knew she had been with me all the way; she just hadn't been sure what to do. After all, she lost just as much as I did. We shared our tears and then we shared our love and then we shared our laughter, too. Together, we decided to show our faith in life, our trust in God, and our belief in humor: We decided to have another ten kids. Anyone who will raise two sets of children—from infants in diapers through adolescents with camels—must have a boundless sense of humor. Wouldn't you say so?"

As I considered his question, the scene faded. I was

surprised, to say the least. I hadn't expected the setting, the characters, or the conversation. But my surprise only made the experience all the more believable. When I opened my eyes, the fire had just about burned out. The room was silent. I reflected on Job's message: It seems to me that our childlike ability to play, to experience laughter, and to enjoy positive humor is a crucial balance in this world of adversity. I went to bed and let the experience "soak in."

THE BIG GUYS

The sixties abounded with searchers looking for the ultimate trip. Drugs provided the tickets and Eastern religions offered the maps. By the seventies a deep respect for Native American spirituality emerged. With it came sweat lodges, a return to nature, and even vision quests. For the most part, Christian visions continued to be deplored as primitive or perhaps psychotic, while Eastern or Native American visions were almost revered. If you hallucinated on peyote, it was a good sign. If you had a vision during a sweat, friends would listen with respect and even a little admiration. But if you—while stone sober—had a vision of angels, friends would give you a little distance and gently suggest you see a shrink.

Following my encounter with Job, I began to engage in a more contemplative Christian experience. I had spent so much time reaching out to broken people, or presenting humor workshops for hundreds of people at a time, that I needed recuperative silence. Being an incurable extrovert, I knew that without the balance of contemplative silence I would become all fluff, all show, all mask....and I would be empty within. White, shiny, and funny on the outside—dead within. Success provided a big temptation to take myself too seriously and develop terminal hypocrisy.

So, one sunny spring afternoon, I drove out to the Pawnee National Grasslands of northern Colorado. I parked on a deserted road and hiked along some bluffs from which I could see over a hundred miles of prairie to the distant ribbon of the Rocky Mountains. This sparsely populated, vast landscape makes it easy to feel a childlike smallness in relation to the spaciousness of creation. After two hours of walking at a comfortable pace, I came to a grassy knoll, one that felt just right—a place that Carlos Castaneda might call "a place of power." It suggested I sit there to meditate, contemplate, and perhaps even pray.

An hour, or maybe more, slipped by in wordless silence. At first, my mind wandered around like a puppy, smelling every idea until it finally decided to lie down and rest. I waited, not intending anything to happen. I just waited in silence, the glow of the western sun warm on my face. Through my closed eyes, all I saw was red. Not an angry red, it was simply an illusion created by sunshine penetrating my eyelids. Peace gradually filled me. I yearned to experience the presence of God, but I knew it was not something I could make happen. And then, without warning, the meditation was over. I don't know how you know such a thing, you just do.

As I started my trek back, I felt relaxed and happy—even though nothing but silence had occurred. I wasn't sure why I felt so light, but I was glad I did. Then to my surprise, I perceived (I can't say I really "saw") three very tall figures. Fifty or sixty feet in height. Very narrow, whitish, more mist-like than solid, no definable heads, but basically human in form. Big, very big....and strong. They were sentient beings and they were "walking" along with me. I felt a safe peacefulness, unlike any feeling I had ever experienced in adult life. As I ambled along, I began to laugh, and I shared my delight out loud with my companions. I talked to them: "Hey, guys, how's it goin'?"

Angels. They didn't talk back. Though I couldn't "hear" their laughter, I knew they were laughing. Then they began to play a form of leapfrog across the expanse of open prairie. They weren't affected by gravity, so their leaps and movements were fluid, more like flying in slow motion. Gradually they became more faint to my senses. And finally, they ceased to exist, save in my imagination and my memory. But somehow, they felt more real and tangible than the very land upon which I walked. I returned to my car and drove home, peaceful and smiling. I knew I shouldn't speak of it then. Even when you're a psychiatrist, you're afraid people might think you crazy.

What a wonderful world view. Humor exists outside of us. It is to be discovered—not created—by our human consciousness. The Ultimate Reality, or whatever you want to call Her, has a marvelous sense of humor and offers us the chance to share in it. Angels can play like happy children and communicate their delight to whomever takes himself lightly enough to listen. Becoming like a child puts us in proper perspective to the Ultimate Reality. As a child we can experience laughter and positive humor as a gift of grace, ours for the taking.

Endnote

Whenever I complete a workshop, I get an opportunity to hear from the participants. Often my clearest insights or most important corrections come from these conversations. Either we engage in a formal question-and-answer session or the participants simply come up and meet me. We make eye contact, shake hands, or even embrace. People I have never met before—people who I may never see again—tell me of their triumphs, share personal accounts of some life adversity, or call me on some mistaken idea or prejudice. Those moments are special for both of us. The Light within each of us becomes aware of the other and we share a moment of loving existence.

Our workshop is over. I have talked and you have listened. At times, I even asked you questions but did not give you a chance to answer. Well, now is your chance. Just as my children, my patients, and my audiences have served as my teachers, now you too can offer me your response. I honestly will do my best to answer you, if needed. (The only event which will stand in the way of a personal reply is receiving too many letters.) I would like to hear of your triumphs. When did humor work and sustain you through some painful adversity? I would like to hear your questions and your conclusions about humor, love, and especially spiritual growth. I would like to hear your corrections.

What did I miss? Do I have a prejudice showing? I welcome disagreement, but please don't try to convert me. Like most of you, I welcome being informed, but I don't like being threatened.

I like to collect stories, so please caution me if you don't want me to use your account in writing or in live presentation. Of course, I change names and location to insure anonymity.

I always welcome new humor material. Any jokes, gags, or assorted funny stuff you send will be subject to Hageseth's Principle of Plagiarism. "If you can appropriate good material without quoting the source, do it."

Finally, I would like to know: Did the book help? Did it meet up to its promise? Your expectations? I especially would like to hear from you after a couple months pass and you have let the material "season" a while.

Thank you for your attention. I hope you have had a few laughs. I hope you have learned something. I hope you have experienced some of the peace that comes when meeting the Light within another.

> Peace,
> Love,
> Laughter,

> *Christon*

c/o Berwick Publishing Co.
501 Spinnaker Lane
Fort Collins, Colorado 80525

Notes

AUDIO TAPES

To Expand your Personal Knowledge and Experience of Humor

THE ART AND PSYCHOLOGY OF POSITIVE HUMOR provides a leisurely learning experience using music to nurture the right side of your brain while the lecture portion presents the complete material of Dr. Hageseth's book, *A Laughing Place.* Musician and music therapist Mark Sloniker provides his original music to create a tension-free and magical learning environment. Recorded in stereo before a live audience, the program is reproduced on four ninety minute audio-cassettes. A workbook is included to facilitate your learning experience.

$39.95

AT A HUMOR WORKSHOP is a ninety minute audiotape which compresses the most practical information of Dr. Hageseth's approach. Entertaining as well as informative, this cassette will need to be heard a few times to get it all.

$9.95

VIDEO TAPES

Now that you have read the book, why not see the video?

POSITIVE HUMOR 101 is a two hour instructional video tape teaching the Art and Psychology of Positive Humor. Recorded before a live audience, the program is divided into three easily digestible modules suited to the class room, board room, or living room. Dr. Hageseth presents the essentials of *A Laughing Place,* accompanied by music therapist and composer, Mark Sloniker. Here you *see* the practice of gelastolalia and how the zygomaticus progression really works. Laugh along with the audience as the good doctor shares his bag of tricks for enhancing your personal humor experience.

$59.95

ORDER FORM

Yes, I wish to purchase the following:

Quantity   Price

_____ **AT A HUMOR WORKSHOP** @ $9.95 each   _____
        (single audio cassette)
_____ **THE ART AND PSYCHOLOGY OF**
        POSITIVE HUMOR@ $39.95 each   _____
        (the six hour audio cassette album)
_____ **POSITIVE HUMOR 101**@ $59.95 each   _____
        (the two hour video tape)
                Colorado Residents add 3% sales tax   _____
       Plus $1.50 for postage and handling per item   _____
                                 Total   _____

Payment enclosed by check or Visa or MasterCard (circle one)

Number _____ Expires _____

(Print Clearly, Please)

Name: _____

Address: _____

City, State, and Zip: _____

Send your order to:
           BERWICK PUBLISHING COMPANY
                501 Spinnaker Lane
           Fort Collins, Colorado 80525

(allow three weeks for delivery)